GETTING YOUR SCRIPT THROUGH
THE HOLLYWOOD MAZE

GETTING YOUR SCRIPT THROUGH THE HOLLYWOOD MAZE

AN INSIDER'S GUIDE

LINDA STUART

ACROBAT BOOKS • LOS ANGELES

Thank you to Tony Cohan, Kelly Akers and the 66 Hollywood professionals who've contributed to this book.

Acrobat Books
P.O. Box 870
Venice, CA 90294

Library of Congress Cataloging-in-Publication Data
Stuart, Linda, 1957-
     Getting your script through the hollywood maze :
     an insider's guide / Linda Stuart
     p. cm.
     Includes index.
     ISBN 0-918226-30-9 : $14.95
     1. Motion picture authorship.
     2. Motion Picture plays — Marketing.
  I. Title.
  PN1996.S83   1993
  808.2 ' 3— dc20   92-35796
                             CIP

Excerpt from the first act of BASIC INSTINCT by Joe Eszterhas
© 1992 Carolco/Le Studio Canal+ V.O.F.

Book Design: Marilyn Babcock & Julian Hills

Manufactured in the United States of America
10 9 8 7 6 5 4 3 2 1

First Edition

TO MY PARENTS

Contents

The Players Include...

====

WARREN ADLER, novelist (THE WAR OF THE ROSES)

SCOTT ALEXANDER, writer with Larry Karaszewski of PROBLEM CHILD and its sequel

ANDREA ASIMOW, vice-president of production for Parkway Productions, director Penny Marshall's company at Columbia

GREGORY AVELLONE, vice-president of development for Kevin Costner's Tig Productions

BOB BOOKMAN, literary agent at CAA

MARTHA BROWNING, story analyst for Morgan Creek (ROBIN HOOD: PRINCE OF THIEVES)

DAVID BRUSKIN, director of development for producer Laura Ziskin (HERO, PRETTY WOMAN, WHAT ABOUT BOB?, THE DOCTOR, NO WAY OUT)

JANIS CHASKIN, story editor, New Line Cinema (TEENAGE MUTANT NINJA TURTLES)

HOWARD COHEN, vice-president of development and acquisitions for the Samuel Goldwyn Company

DOUG CURTIS, independent producer (THE PHILADELPHIA EXPERIMENT, BLACK MOON RISING)

WES CRAVEN, writer/director of A NIGHTMARE ON ELM STREET, THE HILLS HAVE EYES, THE HILLS HAVE EYES II, SHOCKER, and THE PEOPLE UNDER THE STAIRS

STEVEN E. DE SOUZA, co-writer of DIE HARD

LESLIE DIXON, screenwriter (OUTRAGEOUS FORTUNE)

LINDSAY DORAN, former executive at Paramount, now president of Mirage, Sydney Pollack's company

JOE ESZTERHAS, writer (BASIC INSTINCT, JAGGED EDGE)

ED FELDMAN, producer (GREEN CARD, WITNESS, THE DOCTOR)

LARRY FERGUSON, writer (with Donald Stewart) of THE HUNT FOR RED OCTOBER

JOHN FERRARO, vice-president of acquisitions for Paramount Pictures

MARGARET FRENCH, executive story editor for Paramount Pictures

LOWELL GANZ, writer (with partner Babaloo Mandel) of MR. SATURDAY NIGHT, SPLASH, CITY SLICKERS, NIGHT SHIFT, A LEAGUE OF THEIR OWN

GEOFFERY GRODE, story analyst for 20th Century Fox

JASON HOFFS, vice-president of development for Amblin Entertainment, Steven Spielberg's company at Universal

TOM HOLLAND, writer of PSYCHO 2, co-writer and director of CHILD'S PLAY, director of THE TEMP

LEONARD KORNBERG, director of development for Universal Pictures

WILLIAM LINK, creator/developer (with Richard Levinson), COLUMBO, MURDER, SHE WROTE (co-created with Peter S. Fischer), MANNIX, McCLOUD, and ELLERY QUEEN.

DIANA MACK, story editor for Imagine Films Entertainment (FAR AND AWAY, HOUSESITTER, BOOMERANG, KINDERGARTEN COP)

MIKE MARCUS, agent, CAA

CHRIS MARTIN, former head of the story department at Triad Artists

NICHOLAS MEYER, writer of TIME AFTER TIME, THE SEVEN-PERCENT SOLUTION, STAR TREK IV, STAR TREK VI

DAVID MILLER, staff story analyst for the acquisitions department at Paramount Pictures

SETH MILLER, story analyst, Imagine Films Entertainment

MACE NEUFELD, producer (NO WAY OUT, THE HUNT FOR RED OCTOBER)

DAN O'BANNON, screenwriter (ALIEN)

FRANK PIERSON, writer (PRESUMED INNOCENT, DOG DAY AFTERNOON, A STAR IS BORN, COOL HAND LUKE)

SARAH PILLSBURY, producer, Sanford/Pillsbury (RIVER'S EDGE, DESPERATELY SEEKING SUSAN)

LYNN PLESHETTE, partner with Richard Green in the literary agency Pleshette & Green

DARRYL PONICSAN, screenwriter (SCHOOL TIES, NUTS, TAPS,)

PAT PROFT, co-writer of POLICE ACADEMY, THE NAKED GUN: FROM THE FILES OF POLICE SQUAD, NAKED GUN 2/12, HOT SHOTS

CATHY RABIN, vice-president of Fandango Films (Meg Ryan's company)

ROBERT REHME, producer, partner with Mace Neufeld (NO WAY OUT, THE HUNT FOR RED OCTOBER)

STEVEN REUTHER, president of New Regency Productions, the company of producer Arnon Milchan (PRETTY WOMAN, JFK, THE MAMBO KINGS, THE WAR OF THE ROSES, KING OF COMEDY, BRAZIL)

LEE ROSENBERG, literary agent, William Morris Agency, Inc.

HOWARD ROSENMAN, co-president, motion pictures, Sandollar

JORDI ROS, director of development for Steel Pictures

GARY ROSS, co-writer of BIG with Anne Spielberg

GEOFF SANFORD, partner in the literary agency Sanford-Skouras-Gross and Associates

NORM SAULNIER, story analyst at Paramount

BENNETT SCHNEIR, story analyst for Imagine Films Entertainment

LAUREN SHULER-DONNER, producer (RADIO FLYER, PRETTY IN PINK, ST. ELMO'S FIRE, LADYHAWKE, MR. MOM)

MICHAEL SCHULMAN, former agent at ICM and now vice-president of production for Summers-Quaid

TOM SCHULMAN, writer, WHAT ABOUT BOB?, HONEY, I SHRUNK THE KIDS, DEAD POET'S SOCIETY

JOHN SCHIMMEL, Warner Bros. story editor

MICHAEL SERAFIN, story analyst at Universal

AMANDA SILVER, writer of THE HAND THAT ROCKS THE CRADLE

RON SHUSETT, executive producer of ALIEN

MARK STEIN, writer (HOUSESITTER)

ROBERT STEIN, agent at United Talent Agency

JEB STUART, co-writer of DIE HARD, ANOTHER 48 HRS.

ANTHEA SYLBERT, partner with Goldie Hawn in The Hawn/Sylbert Movie Co

MATT TABAK, writer and former vice-president of development for Silver Pictures

JAMES TOBACK, screenwriter (BUGSY, THE GAMBLER, THE PICK-UP ARTIST)

MARK VALENTI, story analyst for Imagine Films Entertainment

GINA WAY, director of development for producer Laurence Mark (WORKING GIRL, BLACK WIDOW, TRUE COLORS)

JENNIFER WARREN, actress/director (THE BEANS OF EGYPT, MAINE)

GARETH WIGAN, executive production consultant for Columbia Pictures

SUSAN MORGAN WILLIAMS, vice-president of development for Percy Main Productions, director Ridley Scott's company

LANCE YOUNG, senior executive at Warner Bros

Preface

As a story analyst in the motion picture industry for the past six years (formerly on staff at Paramount Pictures, now freelancing for a number of top production companies and teaching at the American Film Institute), I am often asked if any of the screenplays I've read have become hit films. My answer is yes, but it's truly a rarity if I come across anything worthwhile.

The truth is that much of what crosses a story analyst's desk is mediocre at best, if not just plain awful. Out of every hundred scripts I read, maybe five are worth considering. Though the industry certainly isn't bereft of talented screenwriters, they are woefully outnumbered by people who call themselves writers and turn out nothing but junk. This no doubt accounts for the decline in the quality of films since the Golden Age of Hollywood and the current trend toward remakes—filmmakers turning to the past to find the great stories that are sorely lacking today. You don't find gems like CASABLANCA and GONE WITH THE WIND anymore, just as the Hollywood of old didn't churn out sequel after sequel and run a good concept into the ground. The key ingredients lacking in most of the screenplays I reject are a powerful story, sturdy structure and strong characters. The central conflict is of little or no consequence, the dramatic progression painfully slow. Dull, talky scenes pervade each page, the story hobbling its way to a lackluster finish. You don't care about the protagonist, much less anyone else, and even the dialogue is poor. I often ask myself: Don't these writers know that their scripts are riddled with problems? Don't they have a clue that *something* is wrong when the 10th draft of the same script, circa 1987, is given the boot? Unfortunately, many writers are in the dark about their own shortcomings, and what it ultimately boils down to is that *they do not know their craft.*

In writing this book, it is my hope to help elevate the quality of screenwriting by conveying to writers how their work is being evaluated, why it's being rejected, and what a screenplay needs to succeed. With insights from executives, producers, agents, writers and story analysts, this book sends an urgent message to new and struggling writers: Whip your work into shape before it comes under the scrutiny of someone like myself. For with the power to trample an inferior script or send a great one up to the executive suite, story analysts can make or break a project and throw major obstacles in the writer's path.

An intensive probe into the literary side of the film business, this book takes you behind the scenes and gives it to you straight: what works and what doesn't. So when you embark on your next screenplay, or perhaps write your first one, you'll have a better understanding of the evaluation process in Hollywood and the undeniable importance of mastering your craft.

1

Who Reads in This Town Anymore?

It seems that everyone in Hollywood, if not half the globe, is writing a screenplay—from the waitress at Spago to the doorman at The Plaza. And why not? A strong, saleable screenplay can be a golden ticket into one of the most glamorous and exciting businesses in the world.

Take Kathy McWorter, for instance. Here's a young woman who wrote a script called THE CHEESE STANDS ALONE about a 31-year-old virgin. When an agent got hold of it the script became so hot that it caused a studio bidding war and was sold to Paramount for a cool million—reportedly the highest price ever paid for a "spec" script (written on speculation with no guarantee of a sale), written by a woman. Writer Shane Black, who penned LETHAL WEAPON, pulled $1.75 million for THE LAST BOY SCOUT. Joe Eszterhas (FLASHDANCE, JAGGED EDGE, BETRAYED, THE MUSIC BOX) racked up $3 million for his sexually-charged thriller BASIC INSTINCT.

But while some of today's writers stand to reap tremendous rewards in the film business, consider these figures:

—According to Chuck Slocum at the Writers Guild of America, close to 30,000 screenplays, teleplays, concepts and treatments are registered with the WGA each year, though the annual number of films released by the studios is about 400.

—Of the 11,000 members of the Writers Guild of America, about half are out of work at any given time.

—Of the 7,800 members of the WGA West in Los Angeles, only 3,900 writers reported earnings in 1991. Of those, only 1,800 were from the big screen.

The truth of the matter is that most of the screenplays submitted to Hollywood studios and production companies are never bought and end up collecting dust on somebody's shelf.

Why? Well, to put it bluntly, most of them just aren't very good.

Either the concept is weak, the characters lack credibility or the story is poorly structured or just plain dull. And the sad fact is that these unfortunate writers haven't the vaguest idea why no one is buying their work. In their lofty attempts to churn out the next blockbuster for Mel Gibson or cash in on the latest trend, they venture blindly into the business of writing and end up with a screenplay that's more fitting as a kitchen table placemat.

But what happens behind the scenes? Who is actually reading the screenplays that flood Hollywood every year? Not the film executives, that's for sure. In fact, the majority of screenplays submitted to studios and production companies are never read by anyone with a key to the executive washroom, let alone the power to "greenlight" a motion picture and send it into production.

That isn't to say that executives never pick up a script; in fact, most of their weekends are spent reading. But let's face it: studio chiefs aren't paid those big bucks to plow through every piece of material that comes into their offices.

Story Analysts are.

STORY ANALYSTS: THE GATEKEEPERS OF THE INDUSTRY

Though ranking low on the totem pole in the industry hierarchy, story analysts can proclaim a script dead in the water and keep it off an executive's desk. We're essentially the eyes of the film executives, who don't read much of what is submitted to them and look to the story analysts to separate the gems from the, well—garbage. So when Friday rolls around and the secretaries prepare the "Weekend Read" list for the executives, the bulk of that list is projects (potential films) already screened and approved by story analysts. Once we put our stamp of approval on a screenplay, you can bet that at least one executive will give it a read. By the same token, we can kick a script right out the door without an executive even seeing it—particularly if the writer is a novice without any clout in the business.

SUBJECTIVITY

The business of story analysis is, of course, highly subjective. What one person raves about, another will reject. So in essence we're being paid for an opinion—but it's an informed opinion based on a thorough knowledge of screenwriting and an ability to recognize strong, saleable material.

We're paid to know story and structure. We're paid to know what sells, or at least looks saleable on paper. We're paid to keep track of the marketplace—the movies, the writers, the deals, the hits, the flops. So our "take" on a script may indeed be subjective, but a number of factors weigh into our decisions. Nothing is (or should be) decided on a whim.

Our job is to read with an eye for the marketplace, not our personal likes and dislikes. If an analyst reads a great slasher script but personally detests the genre, that should in no way affect his or her decision. If the script is strong and has obvious marketing potential, it should be approached as such, regardless of the story analyst's personal biases.

UNION VS. NONUNION

Virtually every job in the entertainment industry is unionized. For story analysts, the union is Local #854 of the International Alliance of Theatrical Stage Employees (I.A.T.S.E.). With the exception of TriStar, all major studios (MGM, Columbia, Disney, Fox, Paramount, Universal, Warner Bros.) are signatory to the story analysts' local. Under the terms of the contract, they can only hire union analysts, who can only work for union companies.

To join the union, a story analyst must work 30 consecutive days at a union company—easier said than done. It's a Catch-22 situation: you can't work for a union shop unless you're a union member, and you can't be a member unless you work for a union shop. It's particularly tough when the union roster is high, meaning that many members are out of work and their names are put on the union availability list. When a union company has an opening for a story analyst, it must first check the availability of the union analysts. Only if the members turn a job down can the company recruit from outside the union.

When I joined the union about six years ago, the roster was low and I was hired by Paramount to fill in for a week while a story analyst was on vacation. I was then able to work the 30 days and was ultimately put on staff.

One of the biggest advantages to being a union analyst is the salary, particularly the overtime. Whereas nonunion analysts are usually paid a flat rate of somewhere between $35 to $50 a script and $50 to $100 a book, union analysts must be paid according to union scale. Based on a 40-hour work week, union salaries currently range from $18.02 to $27.58 hour. With overtime this often translates into over $50,000 a year. While most of the nonunion analysts I've spoken with must read 20 or more scripts a week to make that kind of money, often freelancing for many companies at once, union analysts average about 7 to 10 scripts a week (5 days) and are strictly on salary instead of a per-script basis. And though some nonunion analysts work on salary as well, union readers make the best money by far.

THE WORLD OF THE STORY ANALYST

Over the years I've recommended a number of scripts and books that made their way to the screen—SNEAKERS, GLEN-GARRY GLEN ROSS, THE SECRET OF MY SUCCESS, REVERSAL OF FORTUNE, THE WITCHES OF EASTWICK,

SCROOGED. And while I wouldn't pretend to take credit for these films, the fact that a story analyst responded positively to the projects in written form was likely a major factor in getting them off the ground. Executives listen to what we say; they depend on our gut reactions and our judgment. They'll ask us to read a script overnight and phone them first thing in the morning with a response. They ask, "If you could only make ten films a year, would this be one of them?" Executives often covet what we say for good reason: we're pros. We know what makes a great script and we know what sells. Though no one is right all the time—we may reject a script that sells somewhere else and takes in $100 million at the box office—the bottom line is that *story analysts*, not executives, do virtually all of the reading in the film business and have an astonishing amount of pull.

"In the normal course of events," adds John Schimmel, West Coast story editor for the feature division at Warner Bros., "story analysts have a tremendous amount of power. Just last night, a story analyst called and said he read a script that was spectacular. As a result, three executives read it overnight, which probably wouldn't have happened otherwise."

EXECUTIVES

The primary role of a story analyst is to serve the executives. So if the president of production at a studio has a 500-page manuscript that must be read overnight, it's on a fast track to the desk of a story analyst.

The corporate hierarchy in the film industry generally starts at the top with the chairman/CEO, followed by the president of production, executive vice-president, senior vice-president, vice-president, director of development, creative/junior executive, and story editor. Unlike the small independents, which may have only one or two executives, studios are loaded with them due to the tremendous volume of material being developed and released through the studio pipeline. At Warner Bros., for example, there are currently 4 senior V.P.'s, 7 V.P.'s, no directors of development, and 4 creative execs. 20th Century Fox, on the other hand, has 5 senior V.P.'s, no vice-presidents (they've all been promoted), 2 directors of development and 2 juniors.

An executive's job, essentially, is to bring in projects that can be launched into development: the process of rewriting a script from draft to draft until it is ready to shoot.

Development is the lifeblood of a studio, which has some 80 to 200 projects in various stages of rewriting with the hope of bringing them to the screen. By projects we're talking about any number of things: screenplays, books for cinematic adaptation, treatments, ideas—anything with screen potential. Not all of them will see the light of day, however. Many are either abandoned or wind up in *development hell*—endlessly developed but never shot.

Studio projects are coveted by executives, who shepherd them every step of the way: from the first phase of development, through production, post production, marketing and distribution, to the very moment a film hits the theaters. There's a lot riding on these projects. Executives are under tremendous pressure to develop great scripts that become hit films. One too many duds and an executive is given the boot.

However, once an executive attains a certain level of prestige in the film business, flops (even a string of them) really don't seem to affect their careers. They may get fired before their contract expires, forcing the studio or production company to pay them off (millions of dollars in some cases), but then they typically head for an executive slot somewhere else or land an independent production deal.

When Frank Price was asked to step down as chairman of Columbia, for example, paving the way for the entrance of Mark Canton from Warner Bros., he made millions when the studio bought out his contract and he now has an independent production deal at Columbia. When David Kirkpatrick (once a Paramount story analyst) was president of the Motion Picture Division of a production company owned by Jerry Weintraub (producer of THE KARATE KID), the company didn't launch one successful picture. But since Mr. Kirkpatrick had already established himself in the business among the top echelon of film executives, he simply left Weintraub for Disney, and then went to Paramount as a producer. And since the Weintraub Entertainment Group has closed its doors, Mr. Weintraub has set up shop as a producer at Warner Bros.

THE STORY DEPARTMENT

Before a project is bought by the executives and launched into development, story analysts must first decide if a project is even worthy of development. So when a screenplay is submitted, the executive may not even see it on the first go around. Instead, the executive assistant will typically arrange to have it read by a story analyst before anyone else. While small production companies don't have a separate division for this, the story analyst dealing directly with the executive, the studios and major production companies have what is called a Story Department.

Designed for the purpose of reading and analyzing material for the executives, some story departments also function as a library of sorts, with files dating back to the early days of Hollywood. If an executive requests a written analysis of a script from the 1940s, some story departments (mostly at the studios) may indeed have it on file.

Headed by a *story editor* or *manager*, a story department contains any number of story analysts, depending on the size and needs of the company. Disney currently employs eighteen full-time analysts, while Fox has seven, Warner Brothers fourteen, Paramount eight and Hollywood Pictures twelve. On the other hand Fogwood Films, the production company of actress Sally Field, has a stable of four freelance analysts. Some production companies with offices on a studio lot, such as The Lee Rich Company at Warner Bros., have no need to hire their own analysts and utilize those working for the studio.

A studio story department receives an average of 300-500 submissions per month, considerably more than a small independent, which may only log in 15 or 20 submissions (scripts, books, manuscripts, plays, treatments) per week. Daily submissions come down to the department from the executive suite, most with deadlines. They are assigned to be *covered* by the story analysts, who then provide to the executives what is known as *coverage*.

However, not every piece of material that comes into a studio or production company gets read.

UNSOLICITED MATERIAL

Virtually *nothing* is read in the film business that is not submitted through the proper channels—via an agent, business relationship, personal referral. In other words, film executives are not in the business of accepting material that comes in off the street. In fact, the common practice is to immediately return all unsolicited material to the sender—*unopened*. Granted, some of the smaller production companies may accept unsolicited material, with the stipulation that the writer sign a release form. I've even covered those scripts at the studios from time to time. Such submissions typically come from writers who may have an "in" at the company, have written such an intriguing cover letter or sounded convincing enough over the phone to get their script through the door. But that is definitely *not* the norm.

However, a recent development (according to an article in *Variety*, 9/10/92) indicates that unrepresented writers now have a better shot at getting their work read. Paramount Pictures has teamed with Neufeld-Rehme Productions (PATRIOT GAMES, THE HUNT FOR RED OCTOBER) and Prelude Pictures and, over the next two years, will seek out and develop material by new writers, regardless of their experience.

Says producer Robert Rehme, who's partnered with Mace Neufeld, "Typically, Mace and I have been dealing with very high-profile, top-of-the-line Hollywood writers, who are wonderful, but we've missed being able to work with new writers as well. It's an attempt in an organized way to reach into a very rich area of talent that we normally don't see because we don't have the time. Ideally, we're going to want to make lower-budget material. And they have to be the kind of films that the studio would want to make. We're not looking for art film material."

Adds independent producer Doug Curtis (THE PHILADEL-PHIA EXPERIMENT, BLACK MOON RISING), founder of Prelude Pictures, "We're going to be scouring the film schools. They [the studios] do some of that now, but nobody's making a concerted effort. I don't believe that the studios, because of their need for high-profile material, go after new writers with no track records."

This is a very encouraging sign for writers who want to break in, and hopefully other companies will follow suit. As it stands now, however, the unsolicited material rule still holds for the majority of the business. This is mainly due to potential lawsuits from writers claiming that their ideas have been ripped off, (cries of plagiarism seem to come out of the woodwork when a film hits it big). So it is often a waste of time and postage to pop your script in the mail or blindly call up the studios to say you've got a great idea for a movie. Says Warner Bros.' John Schimmel, "People call every day and say, 'I've got a great idea about my life.' But who cares? Very few people have the time and patience for that, much less care. It's very frustrating, but that is not the way it works." Legally, the executives are at risk to take unsolicited pitches over the phone, and because the industry thrives on relationships, executives tend to do business with people they know or with those who have been referred.

COVERAGE

Coverage, in its basic form, is the industry's term for the story analyst's evaluation of a submission. When executives request that a script be "covered," it means they want it read, synopsized, and evaluated by a story analyst, who will then turn in a piece of coverage. It generally consists of the log line (an encapsulation of the concept in one sentence), a one-page synopsis of the story and characters, and a one-page comment on the strengths and weaknesses of the project. Coverage may also include a one-word assessment at the end of the comment which definitively sums up the quality of a project—PASS, NOT RECOMMENDED,

CONSIDER, RECOMMEND.

A PASS signifies substandard writing and an unacceptable submission. NOT RECOMMENDED is more or less a glorified "Pass"; a story analyst may have found one or two redeeming qualities but is in no way recommending it to an executive. A CONSIDER signifies an essentially strong, saleable submission which, despite some problems, seems promising enough to warrant executive attention. All "considered" submissions are guaranteed to be read by one or more executives. RECOMMEND indicates a top-notch project that should probably be snapped up immediately—terrific concept, near-superior storytelling, wonderful characters, solid writing across the board. A "Recommend" is taken very seriously by the executives, who'll unquestionably read that script as quickly as possible.

Some companies have a coverage category called "Consider Concept," to distinguish between a good concept and weak execution of a script.

At Warner Bros., the readers' criteria are YES, NO, MAYBE, and NO (SEE COMMENT). The latter is still a rejection, but there is enough positive enough about the script for the analyst to suggest that the executive read the comment first before rejecting the script out of hand.

Coverage may also include a box score rating (excellent to poor) in terms of *concept, story, structure, character, dialogue* (see sample cover sheet). A quick glance at the box scores tells executives if a script is worth their time. Needless to say, several check marks in the "poor" column and that submission is probably out the door. The same applies to a "fair" assessment across the board. But if an analyst determines that, say, the concept is terrific but everything else is mediocre, an executive will read the script anyway since no one in their right mind will turn down a great idea, even if it's poorly developed.

Ultimately, coverage is a valuable, time-saving tool for the executives.

Paramount Pictures

Type of Material	Title
Number of Pages	
Number of Scenes	
Publisher Date	Author
Submitted by	
Submitted to	Circa Location
Analyst	Drama Category
Date	Elements

LOG LINE

COMMENT SUMMARY

SHORT SYNOPSIS

CHECK ONE:	EXCELLENT	GOOD	FAIR	POOR
PREMISE				
STORY LINE				
STRUCTURE				
CHARACTERIZATION				
DIALOGUE				

FORM NO. FH-Ra .3 46

Consider these scenarios:

An executive is about to meet with a writer without having read his script. A story analyst reads the script and coverage is rushed over to the executive, who can then go into the meeting with some degree of knowledge and credibility.

An executive passes on an unread script over the phone, quoting verbatim from the coverage: "Well, Bob, I gave the script a read over the weekend, and the concept really is too limited for our tastes at the moment, the story is a downer and the characters aren't at all likeable...PASS."

Knowing that coverage can be a strong selling tool, an executive asks for favorable coverage (a recommendation) on a project he wants to push through the studio system. He's now in a better position to sell the creative group (the industry term for a group of production execs at a studio) on a project.

It's tough to walk into the Monday morning creative meeting and rave about a script, only to learn that it was slammed by a reader over the weekend. This is particularly the case for lower-level executives, who don't have the clout to buy projects themselves and have to sell a vice-president or a senior v.p. on a script before it's sent even further up the executive ladder to the president and ultimately the chairman, the only executive with the power to greenlight pictures and send them into production.

Executives are well aware that coverage can be a help or a hindrance to a project, and they'll use it to their advantage.

Occasionally an executive will read and even buy a project that hasn't been covered first, or one that a reader has passed on. "If the story is interesting, we'll read it," says story editor Diana Mack for Imagine Films Entertainment (FAR AND AWAY, BOOMERANG, HOUSESITTER, KINDERGARTEN COP). "Even if the story analyst blasted the script, I might read the synopsis and if I think there's an interesting idea there, I'll read a little bit of the script before I pass on it."

By and large, however, the executives trust the tastes of the story analysts they employ. It is essential that our tastes generally mesh with those of the executives we read for. If not, we won't last long at that particular company.

MESHING WITH THE EXECUTIVES.

Story analysts aren't given free reign to consider or recommend anything that strikes our fancy. At the same time, we can't be too hard on material. Says Diana Mack, "One of our story analysts was so scathing that it was difficult to know what the positives were in the material she covered. We really like to know both sides."

Executives don't take kindly to those story analysts whose tastes continually differ from their own. Any time we advise an executive to read a piece of material, we run the risk of being called on the carpet. One analyst at Paramount was fired for being too easy on material. Another didn't recommend a script that an executive wanted to push through the system; the executive then asked the story department for a list of everything that analyst had considered or recommended in the past year. Another analyst at a prominent production company interested in mainstream, commercial fare lost her job because her tastes were too artistic.

Such pressure on analysts to mesh with the executives' tastes makes it tougher on the writer, whose script may be read by an analyst who has just been chastised for not being discerning enough. One analyst I worked with was told he was too lenient with the box scores, that he should automatically shift everything in the "excellent" column to "good" and "good" to "fair."

When Lance Young was an executive at Paramount (he's now a senior executive at Warner Bros.), he arranged for each of the story analysts to be paired up with an executive. This put even greater restrictions on the story analysts to gear their tastes to a particular executive, many of whom had favorite genres and were only interested in specific types of projects. After all, if an executive is going to spend a year or two nurturing a project from the ground up, he wants to feel passionate about it.

I remember Lindsay Doran (former executive at Paramount, now president of Mirage, Sydney Pollack's company) coming into our story analysts meeting to discuss what she had in development. One of her projects was GHOST, and from the passion with which she described the love story and the supernatural angle, it became clear what her general sensibilities were. As such, a story analyst for Lindsay Doran would tend to recommend different projects than for Lance Young, who shepherded THE HUNT FOR RED OCTOBER at Paramount.

Executives will sometimes favor one analyst over another and come to trust their tastes implicitly. Other analysts fall into disfavor with certain executives, who arrange to have their submissions covered by someone else. In other cases, attempts are made to match the submission to the story analyst. So if an action script comes in, the executive or story editor will have it covered by an analyst who's particularly knowledgeable or fond of that genre.

THE HOLLYWOOD PROCESS

Now that you know *who* does most of the reading in this town, and the pivotal role of a story analyst in helping to sell your screenplay or cast it into oblivion, the problem then becomes *how* to get your work into the marketplace and ensure that it gets read. You must find some way of placing your screenplay in the hands of someone who can do you some good.

AGENTS

Generally, the best way to launch your screenplay is through a literary agent who is signatory to the Writers Guild of America (a list of agents can be obtained by calling the Guild, in Los Angeles at (310) 550-1000 or New York at (212) 767-7800). A literary agent acts as a writer's representative and performs a variety of functions in the film business—submitting and selling your screenplay, negotiating deals, setting up meetings, finding you work...the list goes on.

Anything the agent sells on your behalf earns him or her a 10% commission. Without an agent, (the Seller), it is extremely difficult to get your script read at the studios and production companies, (the Buyers). "Without an agent," says Lee

Rosenberg, senior v.p. at William Morris Agency, Inc., "I think it becomes next to impossible to get exposure. The daily business of the agent is interacting with the buyers. And for the writer, with the exception of a few entrepreneurs and those who are already well established, there is very little chance of breaking into the system without an agent. The bottom line is finding an advocate for your work who is able to deliver."

You should do anything and everything you can to get an agent. Yes, I know. You've been down that road a hundred times and can't even bribe an agent to represent you. Well, that should tell you something right there: Maybe the work you're showing them isn't strong enough. If you've only written one screenplay that's been turned down by every agent in town, *stop peddling it.* Continual rejects should be a clue that something isn't working.

Because when you come down to it, strong, solid writing will inevitably be recognized and land you an agent. There aren't many great writers walking around who can't find representation. At the same time, if only the brilliant writers found agents, the agencies (if not the entire industry) would be out of business. Not every agency takes on the same caliber of clients. You may not sign with a powerhouse agency like CAA (Creative Artists Agency), but if your writing is decent, there is surely an agent that is right for you. Even if your script has a few problems to iron out, it can be an acceptable calling card to get you started.

Be advised, however, that the unsolicited material rule adhered to by the buyers applies to agents as well.

"We reject anything that is not solicited by us," says Rosenberg. "Virtually every lawsuit that I have paid for over the thirty-odd years of my career has been a result of something that came in over the transom. If a writer is able to find someone who knows me, and that someone calls and says, 'Listen, I have read a script which I think is good,' then I'd be apt to read it. But if the writer can't achieve that level of connection to me, then I won't read it because I don't have the time and I don't want the liability. I'll send it back to the writer with a form letter."

The business is tough. What else is new? If it were easy, everyone would be in it. But don't let that discourage you. If you're dead set on being a screenwriter, get the list of agents from the Writer's Guild and start pounding the pavement. Make phone calls, write letters, send your script around...and DO NOT GIVE UP.

READING FOR THE AGENCIES

Like the studios and production companies, many agents and agencies also employ story analysts, who approach material from a different perspective.

Says story editor Chris Martin, former story department head at Triad Artists, "There are many reasons we read a script, and we cover between 85 to 115 per week."

One angle is writer representation: a script may come in from a writer seeking an agent, and the reader is asked to assess whether the writer is a potential client. In other cases, an agent or a client may want an objective opinion on a script. Other material may be evaluated for a specific star, director, or writer the agency represents. "GHOST," says Martin, "was first submitted to Bruce Willis." Though certain stars and directors have their own production companies (who also hire their own story analysts), often the agencies see the material first and assess its viability for their clients.

Other submissions come into agencies as open writing assignments—that is, projects in need of a writer. The question then becomes whether the project is strong enough to warrant agency consideration on behalf of its writer clients. As it's often said in Hollywood that you're only as good as your last picture, an agent obviously doesn't want to put a hot writer on a minimally saleable project that looks like it's going down the tubes.

Agency readers also evaluate material for potential *packaging*—attaching elements to a script such as stars, director, writer or producer. Packaging tends to increase the saleability of a project and enhances its value to the buyers. If an agent submits a script to a studio with, say, Harrison Ford and Meryl Streep attached to star, that's a *package*, and quite an enticing one at that. (More on the business of packaging in Chapter 2.)

Stressing reverence to the writer, Martin says "It's most important to us that our readers are respectful of the writer whose script they're reading, and that they treat each script as an individual piece of work. If at all possible, we encourage the reader to find something good about the script."

THE RIGHT MATCH

Before your script is submitted, an agent will decide which buyers are most suitable to receive your screenplay. So if you've written a two-character piece about a pair of 18th-century poets, it may indeed be a lovely script but simply too small for a mass audience; it's probably not a studio picture. Or it may have a plum role for a particular actor or actress, but just isn't commercial enough to warrant a buy at a given company. For instance, I was covering material for a well-known actress with a production company on a studio lot. I walked into the office as the v.p. of development was passing on a project over the phone. While it was clear that she liked the script, she termed it a "vanity" project (small, personal, specialized), whereas this company leaned toward commercial, mainstream material. That same script, however, might have been perfect for a small independent with art house sensibilities.

So while everyone is essentially looking for dynamic, marketable material, and many of the indies have gone out of business because their films were too remote to capture a wide audience, not every screenplay is right for every company.

As a story analyst at Paramount, I knew that the studio was primarily interested in commercial screenplays with mass audience potential. So I steered clear of small, arty scripts that were too limited in scope, even though the writing may have been strong. In those cases, I often "considered" the writer in my comment but didn't recommend the script itself. While the studios aren't only interested in blockbusters, current production costs are so astronomical ($25 million for the average studio picture, which doesn't include marketing) that they depend on the blockbusters to stay in business.

So while the slate of films at a studio will differ greatly from that of a small independent, there are always exceptions. HOME ALONE (20th-Century Fox) wasn't a big-budget, star-driven picture by Hollywood standards, yet it has grossed well over $200 million worldwide. Produced by the Zanuck Company and released by Warner Bros, DRIVING MISS DAISY was a "small" picture shot on a modest budget and has grossed over $100 million. TEENAGE MUTANT NINJA TURTLES, released by New Line Cinema, scored big at the box office and became a merchandising gold mine. Says Janis Chaskin, story editor at New Line, "It used to be that New Line was dealing more with offbeat stories, but now we're right in the thick of it with the studios. We can make a $10 million film look like a $30 million film."

By and large, however, the studios lean toward big budget, highly commercial pictures while the small independents, such as the Samuel Goldwyn Company (BLACK ROBE, THE TURTLE DIARY, CITY OF HOPE) and Merchant Ivory (HOWARDS END, A ROOM WITH A VIEW, MR. & MRS. BRIDGE), are more driven by artistic quality.

So try to assess where your screenplay is best suited and map out a strategy with your agent. I remember when Ned Tanen was running Paramount (from 10/84 to 12/88), and word came down to the story analysts that the studio wanted to steer clear of period pictures. At another point, the search was on for sci-fi comedies to star Eddie Murphy. When I left the studio some years later, executive Tom Barad was specifically looking for family pictures. Agents hear these things every day by talking to the executives, who put the word out when they're looking (or not looking) for a particular genre, story, or character. In the end, matching the right project to the right company is the name of the game.

CONTACTS & CONNECTIONS

Now what? All the calls, letters and Hollywood "schmoozing" have paid off. You've finally found an agent, who either signs you to a contract or agrees to submit your script on a trial basis around town. He's excited, you're excited, and your script looks like a winner.

Then something goes awry. You call your agent every day, only to find that no one has gotten back to him about your script, and "things are still pending." The realities of the business begin to set in and you realize that your agent, who initially seemed so perfect, doesn't pull enough weight in Hollywood to get his calls returned. The last deal he made was in 1964, some "B" western, and he marvels at how everyone in the industry today is so young.

Are you in trouble at this point? Yes. But all is not lost.

Landing an agent isn't a signal to just sit back and let it happen. You must take an active role in your career and help sell your own material. Make industry contacts. Utilize any connections you may have. If your second cousin's husband's brother works at a studio, give him a call. It definitely pays to know somebody in the business. Maybe you have an "in" with an executive at Castle Rock. Perhaps you have a direct connection to a story analyst at Imagine or know an assistant at Columbia. Even if you haven't spoken with this person in years, one phone call could be critical to your career. Meet as many people as you can.

Take film classes. Attend writing seminars (Robert McKee's is particularly good—310-312-1002). Finagle your way into screenings. Have drinks at popular industry watering holes. Really work your career. You may not feel comfortable getting out there and selling yourself, but this a fiercely competitive business that thrives on relationships. Networking can open many a door. There are times, in fact, when the only way to get a meeting with someone, much less get them on the phone, is by referral. But, like anything else, it's a numbers game.

If you keep on knocking, someone will eventually open the door.

BREAKING THE RULES

But there are times when even an agent and contacts aren't enough. That's where guts and imagination come into play. When Steven Spielberg was a fledgling director, he didn't sit around and wait for someone to give him a job. He marched onto the Universal lot, put his name on the door of an empty office and went to "work" everyday. His brazen form of trickery put him on the inside and ultimately launched his directorial career.

Now while I am not advocating that you sneak into a studio and distribute copies of your script, or drop them from an airplane, no one ever said that you must play strictly by the rules. In fact, breaking them may well put you on a faster track to success.

In the film WORKING GIRL, Tess is eager to prove herself in the business world, but unable to move beyond the secretarial pool through the proper channels. She breaks the rules by impersonating her boss and risks everything to realize her dreams. By refusing to play it safe, Tess turns her dreams into reality.

You can do the same. Don't wait for someone else to give you a break. Create your own opportunities. Be vehement about what you want and don't stop until you get it. Because if you think that taking the minimum action is enough to make it in this business, think again.

STORY ANALYSTS: ASSET OR DETERRENT?

It should be clear by now that story analysts are a definite asset to the executives. In fact, we do anything and everything to make their jobs easier; and if that means reading until the wee hours of the morning until we're beat and bleary-eyed, so be it. If a book of gargantuan proportions simply must be covered overnight, it isn't the story analyst's place to say no. It just goes with the territory. After we do all the legwork, the executives simply read our coverage and then gauge their decisions based on what we have written. It saves the executive trudging through a mass of reject projects.

But while story analysts are often coveted by the executives they serve, they can be a major deterrent to anyone with a project to sell. I remember rejecting a script years ago, and somehow my coverage got back to the producer (which isn't supposed to happen, but coverage does get around). I was sitting in my office, reading a dreadful novel on the Ming dynasty I wanted to hurl out the window, when I got a phone call: "Why did you pass on my project?" queried the angry producer. Ever so politely, I proceeded to rip the project apart. Suffice to say that the project didn't get made at that particular studio and, due to the negative coverage, probably wasn't even read by an executive. Producers hate it when that happens, and for good reason. But sometimes they're so close to their own material that they overlook significant flaws which are painfully brought to light under the scrutiny of a story analyst.

We can also be a thorn in the side of agents who, hoping to convince an executive to take the first look at a screenplay, have been known to accompany their submissions with boldly-lettered requests: *FOR YOUR EYES ONLY. PLEASE DO NOT HAVE THIS SCRIPT COVERED.* More often than not, however, such requests are ignored, again placing the fate of a project in an analyst's hands. There are times, however, when submissions from top agents with a lot of clout will be read by the executives regardless of what comes back from the story analysts. Maybe the word around town is hot on a spec script by a top-notch writer, or an agent at ICM (International Creative Management) is pressing for an immediate answer on a script in the midst of a studio bidding war. Perhaps a script comes in with a terrific package. In these cases, and others, an executive will read an agency submission that might otherwise go straight to a story analyst. Fringe agents, however, particularly those with a reputation for submitting projects of poor quality, will find the executives far less accessible and wait much longer for a response on their submissions. And if they haven't done business in the past with a particular executive, they have even less bargaining power to steer a project away from an analyst.

WRITER KNOW THY CRAFT

But of all those who fall victim to what one producer termed the "wrath of story analysts," it is you, the writer, who may indeed take the worst beating. While we can definitely be an asset, whether it be sending off a glowing recommendation of your work or offering constructive criticism on how to improve it, the majority of our time is spent rejecting script after script after script.

A writer may devote years to a script, pouring his or her heart and soul into every page, thoroughly convinced that it's a classic to rival the best of them all. Then a story analyst comes along and, albeit with the best of intentions, reads that script in a noisy deli, dribbles mustard on it, and goes back to the office to type out "PASS." Sorry, buster!

Sounds rough? Well, it's a cutthroat business. A story analyst will only be too eager to point up the weaknesses in your script. After all, we put our own reputations on the line when we recommend your work to the executives, and the general consensus among story analysts is *not* to recommend something, particularly if you're on the fence about it.

It is therefore incumbent upon you to *LEARN YOUR CRAFT*.

This will be stressed throughout this book, and cannot be stressed enough. You have to be able to write a decent screenplay. Do whatever you can to become a skilled craftsman and increase your chances of getting past the story analysts.

Don't be in the dark about your own amateurism. Have a friend or relative read your script *before* it gets to the agents and buyers. Better to have your Aunt Bertha give your works a thumbs-down than someone like me who's being paid to weed out the rejects. If your first draft is dreadful, *do not* send it out into the marketplace. It will only reflect badly on you as a writer. Maybe it's going to take nine or ten more drafts until your script is ready to show, but it will be worth it. (I recall reading that GHOST went through something like seventeen drafts before it was shot.)

Word of a clunker spreads fast, and executives are wary about a script that's been shopped everywhere and still hasn't sold. Though there are always exceptions (DIRTY DANCING was passed on all over town and became a huge hit), a long paper trail of negative coverage can trample a project into the ground.

Do your homework and master your craft. It's the best advice I can give.

2

Don't Give 'Em a Chance To Say No

If you're a writer who doesn't write for the marketplace, who doesn't keep track of what pictures are being released and those in the making, then getting your script through the Hollywood maze won't play a major part in your decision-making process. Maybe you're an iconoclastic writer who says "The hell with Hollywood! I'm writing my own kind of scripts, raising my own money and shooting my own movies!" Well, more power to you.

But if you choose to play the Hollywood game—if you're ready to send your "baby" into the belly of the beast—you must realize that even with the best of intentions, whoever reads your screenplay is looking for a reason to pass on it. The onus is on you to give 'em a reason not to say no.

GOOD WRITING IS INSTINCTIVE

The top writers I've spoken with aren't locked into craft and form when creating characters and writing a story. To them, good writing is more than just following the rules.

Says novelist Warren Adler (THE WAR OF THE ROSES), "Good writers know where story and characters come from—the subconscious. They know it instinctively. Following certain formulaic guidelines can be done, as in writing for television, but you're not going to get anything inspired. Why has Shakespeare's work been sustained for some 400 years? Because he had an *instinct for human behavior*. That's the key to a writer's success. If he doesn't know it instinctively, all the craft in the world doesn't mean shit."

Screenwriter James Toback (BUGSY, THE GAMBLER, THE PICK-UP ARTIST) feels that conforming to a preordained set of rules for writing is as foreign to him as "writing in Swahili with my left foot." He writes instinctively and often improvisationally. "Sometimes I'll write a step outline if I can see the events in advance. If I can't, I'll just write the story from moment to moment: Where is he going? What is she doing? Then what happens? Follow it through. All of these things become suggested by the writing itself, much like life. You sort of improvise your way into and out of one situation after another with an instinct for having some kind of goal in mind."

Given the vast amount of inadequate material, however, it is all too clear that many screenwriters simply don't have an innate feel for the work they're doing. Little or nothing they've instinctively chosen to put on the page works. And though they have clearly made the right choices from *their* point of view, the sobering fact is that the trained eye will spot the weaknesses immediately and discard the script.

Literary agent Lee Rosenberg sums it up this way: "If a writer's instincts are good, you'll get good work. But if the genes aren't there to propel that instinct in the first place, you just won't get anything."

HAVE AN ORIGINAL VOICE

The term "original voice" has come up time and again in my talks with people in the industry.

"Originality of vision is important," says Warner Bros. story editor John Schimmel. "The things that are getting bought here have, by and large, a really unique voice or point of view—an entirely original take on its subject matter. We have something in production which has a cop and a bad guy, which we've all seen a lot of, but nobody has ever seen a movie like this—ever. It completely breaks away from the formula."

In my discussions with buyers, all say they're on the lookout for fresh, new material—a complete departure from what they've seen before. A strong, original voice will not go unnoticed in this business.

Says Geoff Sanford, a partner in the literary agency Sanford-Skouras-Gross and Associates, whose clients include Ron Shelton (BULL DURHAM, WHITE MEN CAN'T JUMP), Zachary Sklar (JFK), and Richard Price (THE COLOR OF MONEY), "I have never signed a client because I thought I could make money or thought I could sell a script. What I look for in writing is a strong narrative voice—a unique, passionate evocation of characters, plot and dialogue that innately feels powerful."

At the same time, some material may be too far afield for studio sensibilities. The majors are targeting mainstream audiences, and do not typically vie for material with limited appeal—no matter how original it may be.

"Startlingly fresh yet comfortably familiar," says writer Mark Stein (HOUSESITTER). "That's what Hollywood looks for. I'm a very unique writer. I have a quirky, loopy sense of humor and my own voice, which is good and bad. Because Hollywood doesn't want a voice that is *too* original. It wants an original voice that is, say, just like PRETTY WOMAN or THE PLAYER. When Imagine approached me to write HOUSESITTER, they said the idea was along the lines of RISKY BUSINESS."

That is why you don't see films like KAFKA being developed by the studios, because they're too specialized for general audiences. And if your brand of originality is exceedingly dark, cerebral and inaccessible to the average moviegoer, your screenplays will have a much tougher time finding a home within the Hollywood mainstream.

As writer Frank Pierson (PRESUMED INNOCENT, DOG DAY AFTERNOON, A STAR IS BORN, COOL HAND LUKE) explains, "Nobody is aiming to make a movie that's going to lose money, but the problem right now is that the major players are making a very narrow range of pictures aimed at the broadest possible audience. That's why there are so damn many bad movies. There's also a smaller pool of capital and number of companies that are interested in investing in the riskier niche market. Years ago the major studios would put out a number of pictures aimed at a restricted or specialized market, but they're not interested in doing that anymore. It's become a far more commercialized operation."

This puts writers in a rather unsettling position. You want to be original, yet not so far over the edge that you can't get a foothold in the business. But take heart. A number of very successful careers have been launched not by a sale, but by a solid, professional script.

WRITING FOR RECOGNITION INSTEAD OF A DEAL

"A writer's concern shouldn't be getting your first script made as much as getting yourself known," says literary agent Bob Bookman at CAA. "If any script gets made it's a miracle, much less one from a first-time writer. I would be more concerned with getting people to know my writing; you will get jobs based on having written a good script, even if it's not filmable."

"Have a terrific calling card," says Geoff Sanford. "All of the writers I represent who have been successful have had spectacular writing samples that didn't get made. They were calling cards that got them a lot work, made them a lot of money, and launched their careers. Then they started to get things made."

To those who aren't eager to play the game, this line of thinking is no doubt comforting. Moreover, not all writers get sucked into the Hollywood dealmaking machine.

Says writer James Toback, "I have avoided what is the most lucrative game you can play, that being the auctioning of my scripts to the highest bidder." With the exception of BUGSY, and a recently signed deal to write a script for Simpson/Bruckheimer, Toback has orchestrated his writing career more as an entrepreneur than a Hollywood dealmaker.

"I exist parallel to that process," says Toback, "and would more likely be a vagabond or a criminal than be part of that."

So the bottom line is to turn out the best work you can. And if the script isn't viable from a studio perspective, the strength of the writing may still be acknowledged.

Explains Paramount story analyst Norm Saulnier, "If you read something that's really well done, but it feels like 90% of the population couldn't give a hoot because it's really specialized or too intellectual, you say 'Consider' anyway because, at the very least, you're pointing the executives to a good writer."

DON'T TURN IN AN UNFINISHED SCRIPT

It has been said that writing is rewriting, and this is particularly true in Hollywood. Because so few screenplays are bought—let alone made—in comparison to the number of submissions to the studios and production companies, your script must be in the best shape it can be.

"Rewriting is the name of the game," says screenwriter Leslie Dixon (OUTRAGEOUS FORTUNE). "Anybody who writes a first draft and thinks it's brilliant and perfect is never going to make it in this business."

"Don't turn in a script that you don't think is finished," says Warners' John Schimmel. "That isn't to say that it won't go through the development process, but don't just whip out a script and not rewrite it. Give it to friends, hear it read. A writer needs to take a script as far as he can before turning it in."

"I don't think you should let a script go before it's ready," says screenwriter Darryl Ponicsan (NUTS, TAPS, SCHOOL TIES). "That is a failing for a lot of writers. You have to wait until you're really convinced that you've got something special. And if you truly have something special, there'll be no problem getting anyone to read it."

"I've read scripts without endings," says Michael Serafin, a story analyst for Universal. "When a script is submitted for evaluation, it can only help the writer if it's as close to a finished copy as she can make it. Sometimes I'll get scripts with a note attached, 'This obviously isn't the finished draft, but we hope you get the idea.' Well, I don't get the idea. I have so much work to do, and if a writer can't take the time to finish a script, I'm not going to take very much time reading it. I'll read it, but I doubt I'll like it."

So unless you're hired to write a screenplay and have a deadline hanging over your head, *don't rush it*. Don't have the attitude that a quick first draft will sell and the studios can just make it better. This is an extremely risky practice. Chances are your first draft *isn't* ready to show and you're just opening the door for a rejection.

AVOID CUTE, FANCY COVERS

As most anyone who reads screenplays for a living will tell you, the ones that come in with fancy covers are typically the worst scripts. In fact, they're often laughed at.

"Any script with a picture on the front is usually an amateur's work," says Michael Serafin. "Some scripts may come in like that from an agent as part of a promotional campaign—sort of done tongue-in-cheek—but you know it's a professional writer. Otherwise if a script comes in with even the tiniest drawing on it, we're probably looking at a neophyte."

Serafin also encourages writers to avoid including pictures of the characters and lists of people who should play the part. "I read one script not too long ago, and an actor the writer recommended was dead!"

Turn in a crisp, professional looking script with either a plain cover (black is a good choice) or none at all. Don't draw battleships, flowers or cars on the front. If your story takes place in the supermarket industry, don't send the script around in a brown grocery bag (one actually came across my desk). Keep it clean! Moreover, don't use a cover that looks like you're turning in an 8th grade English report. Don't use a convoluted contraption to bind the pages together. Just use three brass brads and a no-nonsense cover, and have the glint of a pro going in.

31

WRITE A READABLE SCREENPLAY

A screenplay should read so vividly that it excites the reader with each turn of a page. If it's at all slow and laborious, packed with wordy stage directions and a story that goes nowhere, what reason in the world would anyone have to be interested?

"You have to coax the reader," says Larry Ferguson, writer (with Donald Stewart) of THE HUNT FOR RED OCTOBER. "If you accept the fact that when somebody sits down with one of your screenplays, they've probably read 40 of these things already, they're tired, it's 11 o'clock at night and they have to read one more before they go to sleep—that's your audience. So you have to help them want to read it and turn the page."

This is echoed by Norm Saulnier at Paramount who, like other analysts, is often under the gun to meet deadlines and doesn't want to spend an inordinate amount of time on one script. "If somebody writes a script that's hard to read, that takes you two hours to read instead of an hour, there's something about it that you resent. I mean, if it's a great story, and everything about it is great, the characters are great—you're still going to say 'consider.' But if a script is borderline and you had a hard time getting through it—that script has a lesser chance of acceptance."

If you're writing an action script, for example, don't go overboard on describing each chase sequence, shoot-out and explosion. Don't fill, say, eight pages describing every single movement the hero makes in battling the villain. This only makes it harder to get through the script.

"I think each page needs to be crafted," says Ferguson, "and very few writers do that. After you've written a page, look at it and say, 'Does the way this page is laid out cause the reader to turn it to see what's coming next?' In a lot of scripts I've read, I'll turn the page and see nothing but dense stage directions, and they're packed so tight, with no paragraph breaks, that I just don't read them. I find myself skimming on down to the dialogue."

In other words, *write lean!* Be aware of how your script flows on the page. Cut down on the verbosity and unnecessary description. The only time we need to know a character's wardrobe or what a room looks like is if it's absolutely integral to the script. Remember, pacing is key.

Adds Saulnier, "The script that reads so much smoother than all the others—one that really flows—it stands above."

VISUALITY

Your script should also have a strong visuality, painting clear and vivid images in the reader's head.

"Always ask yourself if you can find a stronger, more specific verb," says Ferguson. "People don't just enter a room; they *storm* in, they *bang* in, they *creep* in, they *crawl* in. Emphasize the visual.

"And when you get to the bottom of a page, what do you cut to? Do you cut to INT. PONTIAC-NIGHT? No. You cut to a GLOVED HAND (paragraph break) pulling a .45 out of a glove compartment inside a Pontiac in the dead of night. You cut to the *visual* image. You keep trying to create visual images in the eye of the person who's reading it."

But as explained by writer Frank Pierson, there is a difference between writing a screenplay to sell and one to shoot.

"The ability of most people to read a screenplay and visualize it fully the way it will appear in performance is very, very limited. Even some of the finest directors I've worked with were incapable of it. They needed to have [parts of the script] explained to them and read aloud. So even if the finest directors find it difficult to visualize, and make errors in the reading of a simple stage direction, you can't expect much from studio executives who had their beginnings at Harvard business or law school or as an agent.

"So what I basically end up doing is writing two screenplays: one is virtually a sales document [for the executives]. But once you get a director and actors on board—unless I'm directing the picture myself—I throw out about half of what I've written— almost all the description, and certainly anything that describes the character's inner feelings. The actors and director have to discover that for themselves in performance. That is their creation."

The writer, then, must strike a balance between what is textually concrete and visually resonant. If you tip too far in either direction, you run the risk of being too wordy or not explanatory enough. And while a script is ultimately written for the screen, it must initially be read and clearly understood.

FORMAT

I can't tell you the number of screenplays I've read that are poorly typed and formatted, filled with misspelled words, bad grammar and punctuation—all dead giveaways of a sloppy, amateurish writer. I've even read scripts without periods at the ends of sentences. Granted, you might come across a brilliant screenplay that looks like a chicken wrote it, but the vast majority of the good, solid scripts that sell in Hollywood are not sloppily thrown together.

In my own work as a story analyst, I am always concerned about displaying my knowledge and credibility whenever possible. There is a certain form to follow when writing coverage, and I never want to look like an amateur because I haven't bothered to learn or adhere to it. So should you have the same attitude.

Says story analyst Michael Serafin, "My experience has been that people who send in [formatically] lazy scripts don't turn out interesting material. Form and content are interwoven."

If you're not familiar with script form, *take the time to learn it! It matters!* Learn the correct placement of stage directions, dialogue, character names, etc. People who read scripts day in and day out respond best to what is collectively viewed as proper screenplay form.

"Have decent sized margins," says Saulnier. "Don't try to cram huge amounts of description on a page just so the script doesn't run over 120. Because if those 120 pages, printed normally, would have been 145, it's too long. A screenplay should be presented nicely; I mean, a writer may not have a lot of money, but some cheap computer printers can make a screenplay look as if it were written in hieroglyphics. It's like [the writers] have a knock against them before you've even read page one."

Study books that explain form. Study good screenplays. If you live in Los Angeles, the library of the Writers Guild has hundreds of screenplays on file that can be read (but not copied) on the premises. Others are available in bookstores or mail order services that send scripts right to your home. Here are a few I've discovered based in Los Angeles that take orders from just about anywhere: *Script City* (800-676-2522), which has over 10,000 titles; *Book City Collectibles* (800-4-CINEMA), which lists about 2,500 titles; *Larry Edmunds Book Store* (213- 463-3273), a long-time staple among show biz stores.

So if you don't know how a screenplay is written, don't take for granted that just any way is fine. You must present your work in as polished and professional a form as possible. It's part of the business of screenwriting and should be taken very seriously.

WHAT HOLLYWOOD LOOKS FOR

Submissions are made to the studios and production companies in various forms: standard scripts, books for cinematic adaptation, writing samples, treatments, plays. Before anything is evaluated, accepted or rejected, the person reading it must know from what angle to approach it.

THE SCRIPT SUBMISSION: SHOULD WE MAKE THIS MOVIE?

The majority of submissions to buyers are screenplays, which must meet a variety of qualifications based on the fundamental components of screenwriting: concept, story, structure, character dialogue (each discussed below in separate chapters).

As a story analyst, these are some of the many questions I ask myself in the course of reading a screenplay for possible sale:

Concept
—Is this a high concept project? One with a commercial hook? Is it striking, extraordinary, fresh, imaginative?
—Has it already been done?
—Does it have mass appeal or blockbuster potential?
—Is it better suited to the art house circuit? Is it too small in scope for a studio picture?

—Have similar ideas already done well in the marketplace?

—Is it strong enough to warrant a buy if a poorly written script?

—Does it provide a solid foundation on which to build a motion picture?

—Does it have solid marketing potential? Can the studio or production company sell it to the audience?

Story: What It's About

—Does it hook me within the first 5 to 15 pages? Does it immediately capture my attention?

—Is the central conflict strong and clearly defined? Is it clear what the story's about?

—Are the stakes of the story high enough to make it compelling?

—Does the world of the story (setting or milieu) offer enough for the big screen?

—Do I like what the story's about? What it says? What it means?

—Might it offend a certain segment of the population?

—Is it racially biased or morally reprehensible?

—Is it sexist or misogynistic?

—Does it contain elements that will draw an audience into the theaters?

—Is this an extraordinary story, or rather a simple, ordinary plot with some extraordinary touches?

—Is there a strong emotional pull? Do I laugh, cry, get angry, feel happy? Do I genuinely care what happens from page to page?

—Is it credible? Plausible? Logical?

—Is it timely, or dated? Does it offer something for today's audience?

—Is there a subplot, or more? Does it intersect with the main plot, creating more narrative complexity and affecting the life of the protagonist, or does it dangle in the middle of nowhere and could just as well be out?

Structure: How It's Told

—Is the structure appropriate to the genre?

—Is there a clear-cut beginning, middle and end?

—Does the first act set up the central conflict, establish what the protagonist wants and what he or she is up against?

—Does the second act build? Is there an increasing sense of jeopardy, urgency, tension?

—Does the third act solve the central conflict?

—Are there climaxes at the end of each act?

—Is there sufficient conflict throughout?

—Does the script move, build, intensify, continually hold attention? Is the dramatic progression strong?

—Is there a logical, causal connection between each scene?

—Is there enough new information, or does repetition set in?

—How is the exposition handled? Is it conveyed through conflict, or stagnant dialogue?

—Is the plotting predictable, obvious? Too simplistic or complex? Too vague, disjointed?

—Is the script cohesive? Does it gel? Does it flow?

—Is it written with clarity?

—Does the resolution tie up any and all loose ends? Is too much left to the audience's imagination?

—If the ending is predictable, is the inevitable delayed as creatively and imaginatively as possible? Is the ending too pat and trite?

—Is there a satisfying payoff? Does the writer reward the audience for paying attention?

Character

—Is the protagonist likeable, sympathetic, empathetic, identifiable? Will an audience locate the story's center of good in this protagonist?

—Is s/he an engaging, credible, dynamic character who can carry a picture? Is s/he worth watching for two hours?

—Is it a star role, perhaps suited to one in particular?

—Is the protagonist launched in quest of a specific goal? Is this goal strong enough to hook and hold an audience throughout?

—Does the protagonist fight for what s/he wants amidst conflict, forced to take greater and greater actions?

—Is he active or reactive?

—Does s/he have the will and capacity to continue the struggle?

—Do I root for this character to succeed? Do I care? Do I become enmeshed in his world?

—Does the protagonist sufficiently "arc" through the story? Does s/he undergo a significant change by the story's end?

—Is the antagonist (or forces of antagonism) strong enough to challenge the protagonist and continually thwart his or her efforts? Throw sizable obstacles in the protagonist's path?

—Is the villain a truly formidable foe? Sufficiently bad, evil, dangerous, frightening? Does he make it too easy for the protagonist?

—How are the secondary characters handled? Are they colorful and fresh, or cliched stereotypes? What purpose do they serve in connection to the protagonist? Has the writer maximized the opportunity for conflict?

—How are the characters revealed? Via action or dialogue? Do they mostly sit around talking about themselves and each other?

—Do all of the main characters have individual traits, quirks, idiosyncrasies? Are they true standouts or just average? What are their strengths and weaknesses as far as their viability for the screen?

Dialogue

—Is it believable, witty, intelligent? Compelling, sparkling, razor sharp?

—Is it wordy, stilted, artificial? Hackneyed, contrived, flat?

—Is it coherent? Too rambling or nonsensical?

—Is it consistently well-suited to each character?

—Does each character have her own manner of speaking?

—Is the dialogue too expository?

—Is it too "on-the-nose," revealing exactly what everyone

means, thinks and feels?

—Does the dialogue lack subtext? Is there no other meaning beneath the lines themselves?

—Does the dialogue artfully and seamlessly reveal character?

—Are there too many long, dull speeches?

—Is the dialogue crisp and well-paced?

—Does the writer rely too heavily on dialogue to propel the story?

—Is the dialogue too profane or sexually explicit? Crude or offensive?

—Is it appropriate to the genre, adding humor to a comedy or tension to a drama? Is it consistent?

TO AVOID THE DREADED "PASS"

As discussed, if a screenplay meets most of the above requirements, it has development/screen potential. To avoid a PASS, then, a script must either be conceptually viable, contain some other striking element (such as wonderful characters), be written exceptionally well—or all of the above.

THE WRITING SAMPLE: SHOULD WE HIRE THIS WRITER?

A writing sample is a calling card that showcases a writer's talent. The question, then, isn't whether or not to buy the screenplay but should we hire this writer to: rewrite a development project, develop his or her own projects, "doctor" a troubled script, punch up dialogue, enhance character...the list goes on. Depending on the needs of the studio or production company and the caliber of the writer, a writing sample has various functions in the film industry.

In the case of a development project, a studio will sometimes buy a script but choose to hire another writer—or a series of writers. Though Writers Guild regulations stipulate that the original writer cannot be replaced until after she turns in the first draft, there are times when the original writer just isn't cutting it. The search is then on for a new writer and word goes out to the agents, who then submit writing samples of their clients' work that best fit the requirements outlined by the executives.

So if Universal is looking to put a writer on a female buddy comedy, for example, the executive in charge of that project will receive from the agents a slew of female-oriented comedies to be evaluated in terms of the quality of the writing. Does the writer excel in this particular genre? Do the characters come to life on the page? Does the writer know structure? Does the story work? Is the dialogue crisp and believable? Concept isn't a factor in this case, the executives are not concerned with the saleability of the sample but whether the writer can write and is well suited to the project in question.

Executives will alert the story analysts that a search is on for a specific project. We'll then read the samples with an eye toward that project and evaluate the writing accordingly. If the project is a feature, it's best that the samples be full-length screenplays. It's always questionable when an agent sends a half-hour television script as a sample for a two-hour motion picture. The two formats couldn't be more different, and the ability to write an episode of MURPHY BROWN isn't evidence enough that a writer can successfully tackle a full-length screenplay.

This can be an easy out for a story analyst, who may come across a passable TV writing sample but, not quite comfortable with considering the writer for a feature, say something like: "Despite this writer's ability to plug into a running television show with pre-established characters, there isn't enough indication in this 45-page sitcom that the writer can build a screenplay from the ground up."

The same can be said for a one-hour television script submitted as a sample for features. Maybe the writer has a decent NORTHERN EXPOSURE spec, but, again, the question becomes how well she or he would handle a feature.

If the TV sample is downright spectacular, however, that will not go unnoticed by film executives. Even if it's written on a paper bag, no executive will snub his nose at superlative writing. Besides, some great screenwriters have crossed over from the TV side, notably James L. Brooks, co-creator with Allan Burns of THE MARY TYLER MOORE SHOW, and writer/director of

TERMS OF ENDEARMENT and BROADCAST NEWS.

As mentioned, a writing sample need not be submitted solely for an open writing assignment (a specific project in need of a writer). Often an agent will submit a sample simply to familiarize the executives with a writer's work. If the response is positive, the writer may be taken under an executive's wing and kept on hand for suitable projects.

In other cases, writing samples display a feel for a particular genre, or show strength in certain areas. Says Paramount executive story editor Margaret French, as an example, "It's rare that you find three-dimensional characters in a writing sample, and when you do, it's obvious that that's a writer to work with."

Though the ideal situation is finding a writer who can do it all and do it well, writers with a specified talent may be hired for their technical expertise to improve a specific part of a script. Maybe some strong action scenes are needed, or the ending needs revamping. Perhaps the dialogue needs more spark or the characters need fleshing out. A writer may be needed to enhance a script comedically.

Some of these writers are found through writing samples, though another vital resource to the executives is a writers list.

WRITERS LISTS

As much of their world revolves around written material in one form or another, film executives must have a handle on the screenwriting community from the high-priced script doctors to the newcomers fresh out of cinema school. There are various brands of writers, each bringing to a project his or her own unique skills and sensibilities.

Jeb Stuart (DIE HARD, ANOTHER 48 HRS.), for instance, is known as a top action/thriller writer, while the team of Lowell Ganz and Babaloo Mandel (MR. SATURDAY NIGHT, A LEAGUE OF THEIR OWN, CITY SLICKERS, PARENTHOOD, SPLASH, NIGHT SHIFT) is known for comedy.

To keep abreast of the vast array of writing talent, executives compile writers lists which essentially categorize writers by who they are and what they do. Under each writer's name is often a blurb on what they do best ("This writer is particularly adept at broad, wacky comedy..."), along with their credits, both *produced* (screenplays which have been shot) and *unproduced* (not shot).

Writers lists are continually updated as deals are made and pictures released. Writers ascend and descend in status and new writers burst onto the scene. Writers lists are invaluable to the executives, many of whom compile their own personal lists in addition to departmental or company lists. Studios compile huge writers books as thick as dictionaries, the writers categorized in various ways—"A" list/million-dollar writers, new writers, young writers, writers over 40, comedy writers, action writers, etc. These books take months or years to assemble and are extremely confidential, but somehow manage to be circulated on the sly.

Of course, the only writers deemed worthy of these industry lists are those whose work has sold or whose talent has been recognized. These are the *hireable* writers who've mastered their craft and know their way around a screenplay. You won't find amateurs or substandard writers on these lists and for good reason: their work isn't up to par and no one wants to hire them.

CRAFT VS. TALENT

If the term "substandard" applies to you, then you must take it upon yourself to *master your craft*. It's the best way I know to separate yourself from the "unhireables."

"It is absolutely essential to learn craft," says producer Mace Neufeld (NO WAY OUT, THE HUNT FOR RED OCTOBER, among other films). "A producer wants to work with a writer who already knows the general rules of what a screenplay should be. But the difference between becoming a good and a great writer depends on learning craft, then having the talent to take it a step above."

"Not everyone is a great writer," says story editor John Schimmel. "There are a lot more people who want to be writers than who actually are writers. Much of what comes in isn't bought because the person has not developed as a writer. Their screenplays read lazy, they are empty, have no heart. Or they haven't bothered to figure out how to structure a script or to really think who the characters are and what their conflicts are. If the community of buyers is not responding to your work and giving you the same message, it's insane not to think of the possibility that you're not doing your job right. It's time to continue developing your craft."

The craft of writing can be learned, and how you apply it will dictate your success or failure. You must realize, however, that the idea isn't merely to follow a set of rules in a textbook-like fashion. That will invariably result in cardboard writing.

"I think rules are adhered to by hacks," says literary agent Bob Bookman. "The best writers learn the literal rules of their craft, then break those rules and become great writers."

Adds agent Lee Rosenberg, "I think that craft, or form, is a means to an end. Craft is liberating, that's the way it should be viewed. The knowledge of craft enables you to experiment with different juxtapositions and maybe invent your own. But to become a slave of craft is a mistake. Most writers learn craft as a strait jacket, and then it becomes by the numbers and they probably fail for that reason. There's no inspiration."

No one can teach writing talent. But you can learn craft, and that's what will save you in the end. Because once you learn the fundamental tools of the trade (plot progression, act structure, character, dialogue, and all the rest of it), it will greatly reduce the margin for error and lead you to make far better choices. You won't settle for the same inadequacies over and over again when you didn't know any better. And when it comes time for someone to evaluate your work, whether it be a writing sample or a script for possible sale, you'll be ahead of the game.

TREATMENTS

There are two types of treatments: one is a blueprint for writing a screenplay, the other is a tool for selling a screenplay. In speaking with a number of industry professionals, the consensus seems to be that the former is integral to the process of writing, while the latter is an utter waste of time.

Before embarking on the actual writing of a screenplay, most professional writers first map it out in an outline or treatment: piece by piece, scene by scene, act by act. Where is the story going? Is there a concrete beginning, middle and end? What actions do the characters take? How do they grow and change? What are their goals and motivations? Before the actual writing of the screenplay, every inch of it (save for the dialogue) has already been intricately designed and detailed in the treatment.

The treatment is so important, in fact, that writing deals will often include a treatment stage, the executive working closely with the writer to fine-tune the story and characters in preparation for the screenplay.

William Morris' Lee Rosenberg explains that "In the context of an arrangement between a studio and a writer, when the deal has been set and the writer is getting paid, a treatment or step outline is extremely valuable as a tool to examine the narrative structure of a screenplay. On that basis, a treatment is a crucible through which I think every writer should pass."

So from a writing standpoint, a treatment is essential to lay the foundation of your script and avoid ill-conceived, poorly assembled writing.

When used as a means of selling a screenplay, however, a treatment is of little or no value. "A treatment is pointless. Period," says Rosenberg. "It is a bastard form used many, many years ago in a system which is long gone. I can't sell a treatment. I wouldn't attempt to sell it. I can sell a book—I can even sell an outline of a book. But I can't sell a treatment of a screenplay because they're written differently."

While a treatment conveys concept, plot and character to the buyer, it does so in a style entirely different from that of a screenplay. It's one thing to describe what a story is about, and quite another to actually see it unfold in the course of a screenplay—to see how the characters are brought to life, what they say, how they interact. A treatment can't possibly convey the full dimension of a character or the entire scope of a story. It can only paint a picture of what the screenplay will be about, but that is not what executives typically shell out money for. They're in the business of buying and developing full-fledged screenplays, not treatments.

From a sales angle, it is always advisable to write a screenplay (if not a book) over a treatment. Occasionally, an irresistible idea can sell in treatment form, particularly if the writer is well-respected and carries some clout; but such deals are few and far between.

If you do attempt to sell a project in treatment form, despite the overwhelming odds against you, at least keep it short and to the point. Simply give an overview of your story (beginning, middle, end) and a brief description of the main characters. No one wants to plow through a hundred-page treatment laden with tiny descriptions and camera angles. Also, it's important that you convey what the *hook* is—what is so saleable and unique about the project that it warrants a buy before the script is even written. This is almost never the case, of course, but if you insist on going with a treatment, it's better to err on the side of brevity. In other words—pitch it hard, pitch it fast, and leave them begging for more.

BOOKS FOR CINEMATIC ADAPTATION

Whereas a novel is written to be read and appreciated for its literary integrity, a screenplay is written for a purely visual medium and exists only to put a movie in the reader's head. But despite the differences between these two forms of writing, books can also put a movie in the reader's head and have long been a major source of material in Hollywood.

From THE SILENCE OF THE LAMBS to PRESUMED INNOCENT, RUSH, THE ACCIDENTAL TOURIST, BONFIRE OF THE VANITIES, TERMS OF ENDEARMENT, ORDINARY PEOPLE, THE WITCHES OF EASTWICK, THE WAR OF THE ROSES, THE HUNT FOR RED OCTOBER, PATRIOT GAMES, MR. AND MRS. BRIDGE, SLEEPING WITH THE ENEMY, MISERY and DANCES WITH WOLVES, the book market is a *huge* source of material for films and is closely tracked by the film community.

Executives clamor for powerful novels and nonfiction books with great characters and a strong visuality—from the best-sellers to the galleys, books that haven't even hit the stores yet. They scour *Kirkus Review*, *Publisher's Weekly* and the book section of *The New York Times*. They interface with publishers in New York, the hub of the book business, and want to be first in line for hot manuscripts.

Given the cash-rich deals for Richard Price's CLOCKERS (sold for $1.9 million to Universal for agent-turned-producer Rosalie Swedlin) and JURASSIC PARK by Michael Crichton ($1.5 million to Universal, Steven Spielberg to direct), studios and producers can pay dearly to acquire the film rights to books, and literary agents are only too happy to negotiate such lucrative deals.

A best-selling book and star author can add prestige and hype to a film going in. Tom Clancy's name now carries big clout in both the book and film worlds, just as Danielle Steel wields power in the literary arena and on network television for a number of high-rated miniseries. But when the adaptation doesn't live up to the book, as was the case with Tom Wolfe's THE BONFIRE OF THE VANITIES vs. the watered-down film version (script by Michael Cristofer, directed by Brian De Palma), all the hype in the world won't help.

In terms of evaluating books for cinematic adaptation, we come back to the distinction between fine literature and a potentially filmable story.

Says Lynn Pleshette, a partner with Richard Green in the literary agency Pleshette & Green, "I think it's been shown many times that the closer the book is to literature, the worse the film. There are exceptions, of course. I think the adaptation of HOWARDS END [a novel by E.M. Forster, a Merchant Ivory film] is stunning. But more often than not, the books that make the best films are those with clear narratives and good stories—not necessarily the quality of the writing. I have a new book I'm going to go out with (submit to the buyers) next month which is nicely written, actually. But what makes it saleable is that it is such a strong movie story with strong characters. When you read it you just know it's going to be a movie. You know there's going to be a bidding war for this one."

So a book may be exquisitely written, yet lack a prime ingredient in all successful screenplays: visuality. Other books are too interior; the story is primarily in the protagonist's head. Unlike the screenwriter, the novelist can put an entire story inside the mind of a character and focus solely on that character's inner world—what he is thinking, feeling, remembering. Not so in a screenplay. Due to the visual demands of film, a script can't put a character alone in a room for 50 pages and have his feelings come tumbling out. Expository devices (voice-overs, monologues, having characters write letters or talk to animals) can only go so far in a film, which places greater restrictions on a screenwriter than the novelist in conveying the inner life of a character.

The best books for cinematic adaptation, then, are those with stories and characters with enough *visual* power for the screen. Though many screenplays display a beautiful use of language, their primary function is to tell a story via the actions (not words) of the characters.

Selling a book to Hollywood can be both prestigious and lucrative for the novelist. It can also mean watching your book get ripped to pieces to fit the confines of a screenplay. If the novelist is doing the ripping, it's even more painful. Says Richard Price, "Writing a screenplay from your novel is like a cannibal eating his own foot." (*The Hollywood Reporter*, 6/4/92)

Writer Warren Adler explains, "The craft of writing a screenplay is more a collaborative craft than writing a book. The studio makes changes, the director, actors—everyone makes changes, which often results in a bastardization of the original concept. There isn't a single vision behind a film, and most screenwriters will tell you that if you want some control, write a novel.

"I have sold my novels for the highest prices in the history of the business, and I've written the screenplays for these things and watched them slowly get butchered down the line. They [studio executives] hate the novelist to write the screenplay. They say it's a different medium. I have been disallowed from attending creative meetings because they think I'll defend the book, which isn't true at all. I've had to write secret memos to studio execs before they meet with the screenwriter [on improving the script]. I'll say, 'Why don't you let me attend the meeting and I'll tell the writer what's wrong with it?' But the executive says, 'No, you'll defend the book. Write me a memo and I'll take the meeting.'"

Though Adler says that the adaptation of his novel THE WAR OF THE ROSES (screenplay by Michael Leeson) "is exactly what I had envisioned," just as novelist Pat Conroy was pleased with the screen adaptation of his PRINCE OF TIDES (for which he shares screen credit with Becky Johnston), even the most successful novelists have no guarantee that their original work won't be changed through the adaptation process.

"Once you sell a book," says Adler, "it's gone."

PLAYS FOR CINEMATIC ADAPTATION

Plays, like books, come with their own set of assets and drawbacks for adaptation. As plays are written expressly for the stage, often with one set, many are too talky and small in scope for the screen. Long monologues, the bread and butter of the theater, can be deadly on screen. Still, the theater remains a strong source of material for film: GLENGARRY GLEN ROSS, STEEL MAGNOLIAS, DRIVING MISS DAISY, CAT ON A HOT TIN ROOF, A STREETCAR NAMED DESIRE, DEATH OF A SALESMAN, PRELUDE TO A KISS, FRANKIE AND JOHNNY IN THE CLAIRE DE LUNE, ANNIE, MAME, OKLAHOMA!, GREASE, JESUS CHRIST SUPERSTAR and EVITA (long touted to be making its way to the screen).

Whoopi Goldberg stars in the film adaptation of the play SARAFINA!, and Disney is reportedly interested in bringing to the screen the Tony award-winning FALSETTOS, "a heartfelt musical about friends, lovers and families in modern times and the age of AIDS." (*Variety*, June 30, 1992)

Most stage-to-screen musicals, such as ANNIE and A CHORUS LINE, are big, expensive spectacles that take to the screen in a grand, highly visual style. Yet the problem with many plays is how to take them off the stage and open them up for the screen. Plays are often too limiting and claustrophobic for the screen, which requires more pace and variation of action and locales. Whereas the stage can tolerate two hours of talk as the characters move about a studio apartment, the camera must have more to shoot than a couple of talking heads to sustain audience interest.

TURNAROUND

A project in development at a studio or production company that is abandoned is said to be put into *turnaround*. The writer or producer (whoever sold the project) then has the right, within a specified period of time, to shop the project around town for another deal.

If the project is sold elsewhere, the new buyer agrees to reimburse the previous buyer for all costs incurred in the development of the project, including rewrites, interest charges, overhead, etc. Considering that some projects are in development for years before they go into turnaround, those costs can run into the millions. In addition, the new buyer agrees to give the previous buyer a "rooting" interest in the film, somewhere between 2 1/2 and 5% of the net profits, if and when it is released.

There are various reasons why projects are put into turnaround. After a year or two in development, a script may no longer seem timely or suitable to the marketplace, or is too similar to a film that's just come out. In other cases, studio executives may fail to see a project's true potential, only to put it in turnaround and kick themselves when it grosses millions somewhere else. A studio may hire a new production chief who cleans house and gets rid of several projects, and when an executive leaves a company, his or her development projects may be shelved.

But while having a project put into turnaround is no picnic for the producer or writer, it is not necessarily a black mark against the project. "If a script is any good," says agent Lee Rosenberg, "it's irrelevant that it's in turnaround. If I'm a buyer and I see a script that I like, I don't care whether it was written by little yellow men from Mars and is in turnaround from four studios. If I like it, I want to make it."

When I was at Paramount, I saw two development projects go into turnaround that were ultimately shot and released by other companies: BILL AND TED'S EXCELLENT ADVENTURE, which landed at Interscope, and MY STEPMOTHER IS AN ALIEN, which sold to the now-defunct Weintraub Entertainment Group. The script that eventually became NO WAY OUT was in development under a different title at Universal. When it slipped out of that studio, Triad Artists put a deal together at Orion that ultimately released the film. HOME ALONE was originally developed at Warner Bros., which put it into turnaround and Fox picked it up. YOUNG FRANKENSTEIN was put into turnaround by Columbia and made at Fox. STAR WARS went into turnaround at Universal and landed at Fox. Columbia put E.T. into turnaround and it went to Universal.

So the fact that a script is put into turnaround may have nothing to do with a lack of quality; it may be purely a political or corporate decision. On the other hand, many screenplays in development are in such poor shape that they'll never see the light at the end of the tunnel.

Says one studio story analyst (who requests anonymity), "Sometimes I'll read a development project and ask myself, 'Why was this bought?' It makes you wonder how some deals get made. A lot of things get bought based on some scintilla of potential, then a new writer is brought in to rewrite the script from top to bottom. And whatever magic they hope will come out of that premise never happens. Then it's put into turnaround, and somebody reads it at another studio and says, 'This is awful. How did this ever get bought?'"

But when you figure that a studio releases about 12 to 18 pictures a year and has maybe 200 projects in development at any given time, executives take a big gamble and a good portion of those screenplays just aren't going to make it. THE CHEESE STANDS ALONE, for example, sold for a small fortune and, at this writing, is in turnaround.

Some deals are made not based on the quality of a script but to indulge a star, resulting in disasters like HUDSON HAWK. Other deals are signed based solely on a concept, and five drafts later there's nothing else but that.

Other deals get made because executives or producers want to signal the town that they're in a buying mode and have the clout to make deals. And because agents won't send their best material to buyers who continually say no, it's important to let the agents know you're active.

Still others get made because of business relationships, favors, political maneuvers—you name it. And while the majority of executives and filmmakers *do* care about the quality of material and do attempt to develop as strong a script as possible, a given number of projects will inevitably end up in turnaround.

PACKAGING

From our discussion in Chapter 1, packaging refers to an assembling of elements that, when attached to a particular project, increases its saleability to the buyers. So if a producer shops his script to a studio, he's generally in a much better position by going in with a commitment from a star. What was once just a script is now a package—such as producer David Permut attaching Dan Aykroyd to DRAGNET before selling it to Universal.

But while star power carries a lot of weight in Hollywood, even stellar packages don't guarantee a sale.

Even with Harrison Ford attached, producer Ed Feldman couldn't sell WITNESS to Fox. At that time, according to Feldman, the studio had a bias against making "rural pictures" so wasn't interested in a film about a cop in Amish country. Feldman sent the script to Harrison Ford, who committed to the project within a day. Fox still passed due to the rural setting, but it was ultimately a big success for Paramount.

In other cases, the elements could be great but the script is weak and looks terribly expensive to shoot. Unless the script is as strong as the elements attached, a studio is much more likely to buy a package that won't break the bank.

Packages often originate with the agent and, with its heavy-weight client list, CAA wields tremendous power in the packaging arena. But, says agent Bob Bookman, it isn't often the case that all of the elements come together at the same time.

"In over 90 out of a 100 cases, it has been a matter of the elements going in sequentially rather than simultaneously." He sites as an example the film RAIN MAN, which "is always perceived as a CAA package." In reality, Barry Levinson (a CAA director client) was the fourth director on that picture, and, though it starred a pair of CAA clients in Dustin Hoffman and Tom Cruise, each came into the project at a different time.

"So the presumption," Bookman continues, "is that we must have put all of those elements together in some genius, power-mad, predatory way and told the studio to take it or leave it, when that wasn't the case at all."

While packaging can increase the saleability of a project, there is a risk. A studio may like the script but doesn't feel that the attached director is right for that particular project. Someone may put a project together, and word of it leaks out: suddenly it's all over town and the packager loses control of it. Explains Bob Bookman, "A producer who thinks he wouldn't be submitted the project by an agent may get hold of it and try to sell it on his own. Maybe he has an overall deal at a studio and submits it to an executive he has a relationship with. The executive then wants to buy it and calls the agent, who has suddenly lost control of the material, but still has to take the offer back to his client." This is one reason why agents want to keep their material close to the vest and get it out there quickly.

STAR MATERIAL

In their search for star vehicles or pictures to produce through their studio-linked production companies, most stars have their own development executives and story analysts to comb through mounds of material in the hope of finding a few precious gems.

But what is star material? What are the stars generally looking for? Well—any number of things.

Some stars are driven by material with a strong social or political conscience, such as Robert Redford, who executive-produced and narrated the documentary INCIDENT AT OGLALA, the true story of Leonard Peltier, a Native American activist serving a life sentence for the murder of two FBI agents. Redford has also been leading a major Hollywood crusade to free Peltier from prison.

Kevin Costner, meanwhile, is spending $8 million dollars to make a television documentary on American Indians.

And then there is always...*THE ROLE*.

Having covered screenplays for both Sally Field and Meg Ryan, I can tell you that finding a terrific role can be so important that if a mediocre script comes in but the lead character is fantastic, every effort will be made to make that project work. Tour de force roles are tough to find, particularly for women, and when one comes along they grab it.

More often, however...

"Stereotypic, one-dimensional characterizations are the bane of good storytelling," says v.p. Cathy Rabin of Meg Ryan's Fandango Films, "and star vehicles tend to fall into this trap— female characters more than males. And because the argument against Hollywood tends to be that stars aren't attracted to unsympathetic characters, we get an overwhelming number of stories with innocuous but amiable leads or massively heroic and undeniably winning protagonists that have no basis in reality."

That is why many stars develop projects through their own production companies.

FOR THE BOYS offered a terrific role for Bette Midler and was developed at her All Girl Productions, housed at Disney. Goldie Hawn found a meaty role in the mother-son drama CRISS-CROSS, which was developed by her company at Hollywood Pictures and produced by her partner, Anthea Sylbert. DYING YOUNG (starring Julia Roberts) was developed and produced by Sally Field's Fogwood Films.

Another factor to consider is that what the stars want may not necessarily be in sync with the pictures the studios are interested in making. A studio may be going out to stars with a flashy, high-concept comedy, while the stars may be looking for something more substantial.

Says Michael Schulman, a former agent at ICM, and now vice-president of production for Summers-Quaid (the company of producer Cathleen Summers and star Dennis Quaid), "When a star has a company, I think what they're looking for is the kind of roles that the studios aren't likely to offer them or develop. I think stars are looking for projects that are a little bit more complex, a bit more dark. I wouldn't counsel somebody to write that way, but I think the reality is that a lot of stars are just attracted to that kind of material. I think it gives them more to do as an actor and is more interesting to them artistically.

"On the other hand," says Schulman, "studios have their own emphasis and priorities. Not that they're necessarily at odds with those of the star, but studios are looking for movies that are going to make money, and often what they think is going to make money isn't necessarily what appeals to stars."

But what the studios and stars do have in common is their search for good material. Nobody is out to make a flop, nobody is clamoring to buy junk material.

A great example of a script that definitely *did* attract a star is CLIFFHANGER.

An action/thriller written on spec by former TriStar story analyst Mike France (under the pseudonym Jay Garrick), CLIFFHANGER centers on a park ranger who uses his expertise as a mountain climber to rescue his fallen colleagues. Sold to Carolco, the script is being directed by Renny Harlin (DIE HARD 2) and stars Sylvester Stallone.

You stand the strongest chance of getting your script sold and made by writing the best, most powerful screenplay you can with at least one wonderful role to attract a major star. If you can do that, both the studios *and* stars will likely be interested and then you're in the club.

ACQUISITIONS

There is a difference between *acquiring* a project (a script and/or completed film) for *distribution* and buying a script to launch into *development*. Whereas the latter pertains to a studio or production company investing money in the development of a project, which may go through several drafts, just as many writers, and never make it to production, the term *acquisition* pertains to buying the distribution rights to a project for release to the theaters. In such deals, the studio or production company doesn't spend a dime on the project's development; that is the producer's responsibility before the acquisition deal is made.

In evaluating a project for acquisition, a different set of criteria is used than for development. Says David Miller, a staff story analyst for the acquisitions department at Paramount Pictures, "When you read a script for acquisitions, you basically have to assume that the script is done. If it needs major rewriting, a deal is just not going to happen. We're not buying the rights to develop a script, only to distribute it."

If such a deal is made before the script is actually shot, the producer can then take the written agreement to a bank and secure financing for production, after which the producer will deliver the completed film to the studio for distribution.

When submitting material to an acquisitions executive, it definitely helps to come in with a package—a strong indication to the executive that the project is ready to go into production. Whereas a production executive will buy a project with nobody attached, develop the script and then put a director on it and attach a cast, an acquisitions executive ideally wants everything in place before the deal is made.

"When a script comes to me," says John Ferraro, vice-president of acquisitions for Paramount Pictures, "I'm looking at it as if this is the movie we're going to make. You skip the development process in my department; the scripts have all been developed outside."

With certain deals, a script may have been passed on or put into turnaround by the production side and picked up by acquisitions. Says Howard Cohen, vice-president of development and acquisitions for the Samuel Goldwyn Company, "Many of the movies that we've picked up [acquired] we initially passed on as scripts [MISSISSIPPI MASALA, THE WATERDANCE, BLACK ROBE]. It's not always that there's something bad in the screenplay, but more a question of execution. Can the director pull this off with great artistry?"

In acquiring projects that have already been shot, Cohen says, "You can afford to take a chance on certain finished films. You can take on more unusual, adventurous material because you can already see how it's been executed. Certain kinds of movies depend so much on very high quality execution because they're not driven by stars or a commercial concept."

At Paramount, however, commerciality is generally the rule. Ferraro cites as an example the picture JUICE. The script had apparently been submitted to production at one time and was passed on. But the movie got made on a very low budget by an independent company. "They showed us the director's cut and we bought it. Given the success of BOYZ N THE HOOD," says Ferraro, "we felt that JUICE had some commercial potential, and what was a $3.5 million picture went on to make $21 million."

For the writer, then, a script that is passed on for development may by no means be dead. But before you go the acquisitions route, it becomes imperative that your script be camera-ready, and it's best to hook up with a producer and an agent with clout who can help you package it.

GOOD WRITING IS GOOD WRITING

The players in Hollywood aren't always looking for a particular project, role, concept or genre. But they are *always* looking for good writing. So if you can offer that, if you know your way around a screenplay and can turn out good, consistent work, you'll inevitably get hired. It's a given.

3

Concept &
Commerciality

If a script is saleable in Hollywood, it won't be for its beauty as much as its money-making potential. When the two come together, so much the better. But at the studios, the bottom line is always the buck.

Quoted in a *Los Angeles Times* article (4/5/92), Disney Studios boss Jeffrey Katzenberg says, "Hollywood is about the marriage of art and commerce—with the accent on commerce. European filmmaking is about art. Period."

At the same time, there exists a dichotomy in Hollywood between the buying and writing communities. What drives some of the top writers in the business is not commerciality and saleability. While flourishing within the Hollywood system, these writers aren't dreaming up the next million-dollar concepts or trying to second-guess the marketplace. What drives them is *passion.*

Says Gary Ross, co-writer of BIG with Anne Spielberg, "Anne and I wrote a $200 million movie just trying to satisfy ourselves artistically, not worrying about box office. I think any time you worry about that, you're in a lot of trouble. You'll get HUDSON HAWK as often as you'll get LETHAL WEAPON. Worrying about the commercial considerations is no guarantee of commercial success. The only guarantee of commercial success I've found is a strong vision or voice and an emotional experience on the part of the moviegoer."

Says James Toback of purely commercial writing, "I have such contempt for it that I would have contempt for myself if I tried it. So I'd be both bad at it and sick about it. But I'd like to think that even if I could do it very well that I wouldn't be even remotely tempted.

"I am only interested in thinking something through in a thorough way and then executing it. Just coming up with an idea and then saying that is the movie is why most movies stink. To me, writing isn't about making a score."

Says Joe Eszterhas (BASIC INSTINCT, FLASHDANCE, JAGGED EDGE), "I think there's a great danger for a writer to sit down and try to figure out what will be commercial, because you're going to wind up doing contortions. Just sit down and write what you believe in. The quality of the material will be better and you will feel like a writer—not Willy Loman at the end of the day hustling ideas. What you should be concerned about is writing the best story that you can as the muse moves you."

But what if the script is too obscure? What if it's not at all commercial and no one will buy it?

"You will be better off for having written it," says Eszterhas. "That certainly happened to me from a commercial point of view on three scripts I never sold because the marketplace judged that they were either too small-scale or didn't work commercially for whatever reason. So you run the risk of that happening. But I think you're a better writer for having done it and writing what is close to your heart."

But let's be realistic. It seems easier to suggest writing from the heart after you've made millions from the sale of a script. If you look at Eszterhas' most successful screenplays—BASIC INSTINCT, FLASHDANCE, JAGGED EDGE—you'll notice that they have a commercial edge with a strikingly conceptual hook.

That's what the studios want.

Says Leonard Kornberg, director of development for Universal Pictures, "When a script comes in, it is not the writing on the page that will get it purchased. It is the *concept*. The writing on the page will get the writer noticed and pull him out of the crowd. We'll look for his next script and may throw assignments his way. But in terms of a sale, the impressiveness of the writing is not a primary concern. It's secondary. If a script is conceptual but not impressively written, it often has a better chance of selling than something that is well-written but small and not conceptual. The belief is that a script can be fixed and made to work. Sometimes this belief is made in error on someone's part, but if the concept is strong, the first act is there and an executive is pushing it, that can often be enough to get a project bought.

"The movies the studio executives buy and make are not necessarily those that they themselves want to see. They're the movies that they believe there's an audience for and will make some money. And to believe that a movie is going to make money, you must be convinced that you can market it and can get a star for it. Is it castable? If a script isn't conceptual and castable and you don't have strong filmmakers who want to make it, then it doesn't stand a chance in hell."

Adds Jason Hoffs, vice-president of development for Amblin Entertainment, Steven Spielberg's company at Universal, "In the current spec market, most scripts aren't purchased for the quality of the writing but for the quality of the idea. Probably 80% of the spec scripts this year were bought for concept and not execution."

Then as a smart writer who wants to enter and remain in the business, you have to compromise. You may have to sacrifice your esthetic sensibilities a bit to play the Hollywood game, but if it's the difference between keeping your lovely little script in a drawer and selling one for three million bucks—but still a solid piece of writing—which would you choose?

Says writer Leslie Dixon (OUTRAGEOUS FORTUNE), "If you just sit in your little cubicle and write screenplays out of the deepest passion of your heart, you're bound to never sell those screenplays or, if you do, be ground into the dirt as other writers are hired to make them more commercial. If you're writing to exorcise your innermost demons or perform psychotherapy on the dimmest caverns of your mind, you're better off writing plays or novels. Often the most important thing a writer really needs to get deals in this town is a good concept or premise."

You don't find the top screenwriters *only* writing personal stories about which they are intensely passionate. They are savvy enough to know that the business doesn't work that way, and unless they write scripts the studios want to buy, they won't make a dime.

Says Frank Pierson, "You've got to write as well as you can to succeed on any level, either commercially, or writing one of those scripts you're fully satisfied with that you know has about as much chance of selling as a snowball in hell. Those are terrible disappointments in a way because there they are, sitting on the shelf, and nobody's ever going to make them. Yet you know that's some of the best writing you ever did.

"*Premiere* magazine does an annual feature about the Best Unproduced Screenplays," Pierson continues, "and the first year they did that, one of mine was picked.

"It was a script called AIN'T THAT AMERICA, about three unemployed steel workers, that was commissioned by Warner Bros. But it was the early part of the Reagan administration, and by the time I finished the screenplay, nobody wanted to talk about the unemployment situation. Everybody wanted to look on the bright side."

The concept was no longer timely, therefore no longer commercial. By the time Pierson turned in the script, the studio's production chief had been replaced and the script ended up on the shelf. What's more, Pierson says, he's "never been able to get anybody interested enough to pay the studio the money that they paid me to reactivate the script."

Adds writer Darryl Ponicsan (SCHOOL TIES, NUTS, TAPS), "So much of what we see in movies now is just pure entertainment—a writer manipulating character for the amusement of the audience. That is not what I'm interested in."

Nonetheless, Ponicsan is quick to point out that "If you're a player in the Hollywood game, then you're looking for the big score. If you're looking for the big score, then you're dreaming up the exciting concept. And whether or not the picture actually gets made is almost secondary to selling it and making the deal. You're not going to find a small, sensitive piece selling for two million dollars. Lightning may strike if the piece is made, but that's rare. Most of the scripts that are bringing in the big bucks are basically clever derivations of things that have worked in the past. It always involves action, and if sex is there, all the better."

Bottom line: If you're a writer without something to sell, either a viable property or your own talent, grab the nearest lifeboat...*FAST*.

THE VALUE OF AN INNOVATIVE CONCEPT

When I was at Paramount, an executive addressed the story analysts on their search for saleable material and stressed the importance of concept: a fresh, unique, highly marketable idea for a movie that grabs you—an idea that hasn't been done a million times, something you haven't quite seen before. This cannot be stressed enough. No one is looking to buy a script that is merely a hackneyed rehash of what we've already seen. But virtually everyone wants innovative, knock-your-socks off concepts with big moneymaking potential.

"This is a business where people pan for gold," says Jordi Ros, director of development for Steel Pictures (executive-turned-producer Dawn Steel) at Disney. "Studios are going after the mainstream hit, and they know that if they hit the formula right...they may bomb a few times, but when they hit they're going to hit BIG. That's the game they play."

And what the major players invariably want is something new and different, something with an edge. Not too obscure or "out there" to preclude mass consumption, but something striking enough to rise above the norm. If an idea is overly familiar, predictable and formulaic, forget it. It's gone.

Says Steven Reuther, president of New Regency Productions, (the company of prolific producer Arnon Milchan—PRETTY WOMAN, JFK, THE MAMBO KINGS, THE WAR OF THE ROSES, KING OF COMEDY, BRAZIL), "I have the luxury of reviewing some 30-50 scripts a week, and you'd be surprised to find how similar many of them are. What are the most common submissions seem directly related to what was the most successful movie last year. But I'm bored if it's too familiar.

"A script has to be unique in some way. If it's about two cops, what do those two cops do? If they catch a drug smuggler who's coming from Mexico, well... I've seen that three billion times. I'm not interested. I won't read it.

"But if you take those two cops, and one of them is accused of murder and his wife was murdered by a serial killer two years ago, now I'm starting to get interested. Wait a minute...how does this play?" That's how THREE RIVERS (by Rowdy Herrington) started, which is now shooting for Columbia with Bruce Willis.

Of Herrington, who's also directing the film, Reuther says, "He had a really interesting notion of a policeman who had fallen from grace, was obsessed with the death of his wife and a series of serial killings, and never believed that the person who was caught was in fact the killer. All of a sudden it was more than a cop movie for me."

That's the key. Conjure up an idea for a film that transcends the bare conventions of a particular genre and offers more than what the buyers expect.

It is also important that your concept be immediately graspable, easily conveyed in one line. If it takes a long song and dance to understand what the movie is, you're a goner. Executives want to visualize the movie right off. (A perfect example is HONEY, I BLEW UP THE KID. The concept definitely snaps; right away you know what the movie's about.) A great concept doesn't require a lot of explanation.

BEVERLY HILLS COP: Following a friend's murder, a smart-assed cop is led from the gritty streets of Detroit to Beverly Hills.

THE TERMINATOR: A cyborg from the 21st century is sent to

modern day Earth to alter future events by changing the past.

TOP GUN: Flying in the face of danger, a daring Navy fighter pilot is out to become "the best of the best."

DIE HARD: Terrorists seize an L.A. high-rise at Christmastime, and an off-duty cop from New York plays hero to battle the forces of evil and rescue innocent people...including his wife.

TOTAL RECALL: In the year 2084 A.D., Schwarzenegger is up against the dictator of a Martian mining colony with the power to alter reality.

You can pull the concepts right out of these blockbusters and they sizzle with commercial, mass audience potential. That's what the buyers are looking for.

Says Gina Way, director of development for producer Laurence Mark (BLACK WIDOW, WORKING GIRL, TRUE COLORS), "If the script has a really unique, catchy idea that can be described in one sentence, if it sounds interesting and really fresh...we'll buy it."

HIGH CONCEPT

Studio executives often lean toward high concept pictures—those with a strikingly commercial, gimmicky spin and a definite hook. The vast majority are action pictures and comedies, TWINS being a classic example: Arnold Schwarzenegger and Danny DeVito as twin brothers separated at birth.

Continually popular are *fish-out-of-water* comedies, such as BEVERLY HILLS COP, in which a character is taken out of his element and forced to become acclimated to a new environment. Other hits of this kind include: SPLASH (a mermaid in New York City), CROCODILE DUNDEE (a man from the Australian Outback in NYC), KINDERGARTEN COP (a tough cop in a classroom full of five-year-olds), DOC HOLLYWOOD (a big city doctor in a small rural town), SECRET OF MY SUCCESS (a Kansas farm boy in the big city finagles his way up the corporate ladder), PRIVATE BENJAMIN (Jewish American Princess joins the army), THREE MEN AND A BABY (a trio of single guys thrust into the foreign world of caring for a baby), and ENCINO

MAN (a frozen caveman found in a backyard in Encino).

PRETTY WOMAN has a fish-out-of-water slant, and the evolution of that project reinforces the importance of concept. It began with a screenplay by Jonathan Lawton called 3000, a dark morality play about a Wall Street raider and a Hollywood prostitute. When it originally sold to Disney, Michael Eisner (chairman/CEO of the Walt Disney Company) described it as "disgusting beyond belief." (*Vanity Fair*, November 1991) But on the strength of the concept, the project was launched into development. What was once a hard-edged tale became a lighter, funnier, Cinderella-type fantasy that became PRETTY WOMAN and the biggest box office hit of 1990.

A high concept idea also paid off handsomely for a young writer I spoke with who's a "hip pocket" client of CAA: not signed with the agency, though an agent liked his spec script (a high concept comedy-adventure) enough to submit it around town. During a meeting with a top-level producer in search of a new project, the agent pitched him various script ideas, one of which was the young writer's. The concept had such a strong hook that it immediately grabbed the producer, who ended up *optioning* it with the intent of setting it up at a studio (to *option* a project means buying the rights for a specified amount of time for a percentage of the purchase price—say, $50,000 for a year's option against $500,000 for the full purchase price). In this case, a high concept property was instrumental in launching a writer's career.

THE SPEC BOOM

A few years ago Hollywood went through what was called a "spec boom." Many of those spec scripts were the subject of big money auctions between rival studios, and in an article for GQ in July of 1990, agent Jeremy Zimmer said the specs which sparked a feeding frenzy combined "great ideas, castable leads and a commercial smell."

Yet a good portion of those big-selling scripts weren't well-written. Says CAA agent Bob Bookman, "I've read a lot of scripts that sold in the half-million to million-dollar range, and it really depressed me. The writers sat down and came up with a good, one-line concept, and that's what the studios responded to. And while there is nothing wrong in principal with a really strong concept, you need other elements besides that.

"Most of the big-selling scripts were action films, and in the back of the studios' minds were not only concept but casting. I represented a screenwriting team and sold two or three scripts of theirs for a lot of money. They were all very high concept-driven scripts that, in my opinion, were not very well written. Those were the highest numbers that I got for spec scripts, and it depressed me a lot."

Says Jordi Ros, "There is something to be said for paying a lot of money for a really well-written script, which are so few and far between. But a lot of the [high-selling] spec scripts aren't that well written and generally aren't worth the money paid for them."

This may explain why some of those scripts have yet to reach the screen. Take the TICKING MAN, for instance, a script by Manny Coto and Brian Helgeland that sold to Largo Entertainment (Larry Gordon's company at Fox) a couple of years ago for $1.2 million. The concept: What happens when a nuclear-armed robot starts thinking for itself? It sounds hot, and, before it went into a bidding war, there was so much hype surrounding the script that the buyers couldn't wait to read it. To entice the buyers, the agent employed a brilliant P.R. ploy by sending out ticking clocks that read "THE TICKING MAN IS COMING..." (*GQ Magazine*, July 1990)

At one point, Bruce Willis was set to star. But he has since pulled out, and the movie still hasn't been made. At this writing, the script remains in development.

Another example is a script called CITY OF DARKNESS. Written by Joe Gayton and Patrick Cirillo, it's the story of two kids who turn loose a comic book super-hero and villain in the real world. Conceptually striking? You bet. Well, Hollywood thought so, too, and furiously bid on the script back in 1990. It ultimately sold for $750,000 to Columbia Pictures and Michael

Douglas, and the writers became two of the hottest commodities in town.

Where is the project today? Still in development at Columbia. But the key factor is that it offered enough *conceptually* to sell for a lot of money. Whether or not it gets made is something else entirely.

CONCEPT VS. EXECUTION

But if the concept isn't the prime element in the saleability of a script, then there had better be some exceptional writing within those pages. The characters had better be dynamite, the story compelling, the structure solid, the dialogue strong and believable. Granted, one or two of these areas may be lacking and the script still launched into development, but in the absence of a captivating concept, execution is key.

If you take a film like TWINS, which grossed over $100 million, it isn't likely to go down in history as a stunning piece of writing. But then it was never meant to be. Although well done for what it is, the selling point of that film (and others of its ilk) is not the writing as much as a highly inventive concept coupled with likeable, bankable stars.

Take COCKTAIL. Here's a film that put a big city bartender in a tropical resort (another fish-out-of-water concept), gave him a pretty girl to romance and her rich daddy to contend with. CITIZEN KANE it isn't. The story was contrived and predictable. Yet the picture brought in money. Audiences bought into the conceptual formula, the sexiness of Tom Cruise spinning bottles behind a bar like a cowboy twirls his gun.

ORDINARY PEOPLE, however, doesn't hinge on a flashy, commercial concept, but the Oscar-winning script by Alvin Sargent (based on a novel by Judith Guest) is a superior piece of writing. The selling point here (in addition to the stars) is the depth of emotion in the story and characters.

Therein lies the difference. Here are three successful films: two driven primarily by *concept*, the other by *execution*. Both play a critical part in the business, yet don't always go hand in hand.

Says Cathy Rabin, v.p. of development for Fandango Films (Meg Ryan's production company), "I tend to believe that the concept doesn't have to be completely fresh if the execution is. Familiar concept is a non-issue if the execution is inventive and compelling. A lot of 'noir'—pseudo-noir, apres noir, noir-homage—comes down the pike and most of it is pretty familiar and hackneyed. Then there's CHINATOWN, which virtually reinvented the genre through the sheer brilliance of Towne's execution. You could say BODY HEAT was a typical Cain-inspired noir concept, but there, the quality of Kasdan's writing rendered a familiar setup utterly suspenseful and compelling."

So the leeway for the writer can be greater with high concept comedies than for, say, spy thrillers or political dramas, genres more dependent on supremely crafted plots and characters for their success.

Be aware, however, that there are many more formulaic, high-concept comedies that flop at the box office, and it is only with that magical blend of ingredients on the screen that they rise to the top.

HIGH CONCEPT WON'T ALWAYS GUARANTEE A SALE

Though many scripts have sold, and many more will continue to sell for a small fortune on the basis of concept, a number of high concept comedies have been box office duds (MY STEP-MOTHER IS AN ALIEN, MAID TO ORDER, TROOP BEVERLY HILLS, HELLO AGAIN). A writer cannot bank on the notion that every executive favors concept over execution. That isn't the case across the board. A high concept script may land on someone's desk whose bottom line is good writing.

Says production executive Michael Schulman, "I think the biggest mistake a lot of young, newer writers make is they try to write commercial movies. They sort of figure, okay...I'm going to write a LETHAL WEAPON because that did well, or I'm going to write a cheesy horror movie. They use that as the basis for what they write about and how they write as opposed to saying 'Who am I as a person? What do I have to say that's worth saying?'

Good writing is good writing because you feel something. You have something important to say and you have an interesting way of saying it, not because you think you can do what somebody else has already done."

Says CAA agent Mike Marcus, "You can't just depend on concept, in my opinion. I think it's harder to buy concepts. I think you buy execution; you buy what works. Yes, there are always going to be follow-up trends on whatever is hot at the moment, but the bottom line is good, solid stories with good, solid character development is what it's always about."

Adds Anthea Sylbert, a partner with Goldie Hawn in the Hawn/Sylbert Movie Co., "I think it's dangerous to try to guess what is saleable and commercial. I think you can only react to concepts you feel some passion for, some connection to. Concepts don't work for me when they seem too contrived, when there is a lie at their very center."

"It's much harder than it used to be to sell concepts," says Warner Bros.' John Schimmel. "The same reason why it's hard to sell a script on a pitch. It's the same type of crap shoot: the concept is great, but what is it going to look like on the page?"

Adds Margaret French, executive story editor for Paramount Pictures, "Concept can wear very thin after the first act. After that, there must be substance to keep an audience interested. Even if it's a high concept idea, the story still has to be there, the characters still have to grow."

So never assume that conceptually formulaic writing is a ticket to success. Your writing must still be buoyant enough to breathe new life into that formula, which isn't easy to do. But if you can somehow plug into a formula in a vastly entertaining way and offer a dynamite role for a star, then what would normally be passed on for being too familiar could well be considered as having the capacity to entice mainstream moviegoers.

THE COMPETITIVE MENTALITY

There is fierce competition in the film business for high-level, commercial material with blockbuster potential. What one has, the other often wants.

"The agents control the flow of material," says New Regency's Steven Reuther, "so the same ideas naturally come to the buyers at the same time. The reasoning is that if someone else thinks it's a good idea, it must be a good idea. It's nice to hear that people think that what you want to do is viable and are trying to imitate or compete with it."

Adds Steel Pictures' Jordi Ros, "A lot of studios now are developing competing projects, and it's a matter of attracting talent and getting it out first."

At this writing, two Christopher Columbus movies have hit the screen. In other deals...a "Huck Finn" script sold to Disney for $500,000, and TriStar is reportedly ready to take theirs out to stars and directors. Writer-director-producer John Hughes also has a "Huck Finn" project in the works at Fox. Columbia is developing a "Three Musketeers" script, and Disney just bought one for a million bucks. The Zucker brothers (of AIRPLANE! fame) have a "Davy Crockett" project in the works, as does a major studio.

Notice that all of these projects, like THE LAST OF THE MOHICANS, are historical adventures—a cinematic trend likely sparked by the success of DANCES WITH WOLVES. Such pictures are a throwback to the Hollywood of old, and the fact that there are so many of them, typifies the like-mindedness that permeates the studio system.

What's more, the competition can become so heated between studios that one will bash the other's project.

Quoted in *Daily Variety* (June 25, 1992), TriStar chairman Mike Medavoy said of Disney's "Huck Finn" project, "They're making a cheapo TV version. We'll make a film closer to being a classic. It's on the front burner, we're revising our script and we're talking to A-class directors and actors."

TriStar had their "Huck" script (by Matthew Jacobs) in development before Disney, which hopes *theirs* (by Stephen Sommers) will be a classic. Says Sommers (*Variety* 6/25/92), who is also the film's director, "I think we're going to pull off some real casting coups because people really believe this is going to be the definitive 'Huck Finn' and they want to be in it." Sommers is so confident, in fact, that he says "I am Huck Finn," referring to his growing up along the Mississippi.

This competitive mentality was at play when Fox was developing a Robin Hood movie a few years back, and was beaten to the theaters by Morgan Creek and Warner Bros. with ROBIN HOOD: PRINCE OF THIEVES starring Kevin Costner. While both films were made, Fox aired theirs on television with Patrick Bergin.

Says Steven Reuther, "You have to get it out there first, because if the audience has already seen one of the movies, they're already satiated. They've heard that story. If I were in that situation, I would certainly want first shot at it."

For the writer, competition between studios can be a hindrance or an asset. On the one hand, it is a disheartening experience to generate a strong idea and write the script, only to see a virtual replica of it splashed across the screen in someone else's film. What seemed like a novel idea is no longer fresh, and no one at the studios is interested. And if the other movie is a flop, you can just as well kiss your idea goodbye. Such was the plight of a film student at USC whose script, though well-written, was too similar in concept to the ill-fated RADIO FLYER to generate interest.

On the other hand...

"If you're a smart writer," says Jordi Ros, "and you find that a studio has a really hot property that they're going out to directors with, you write something like it. And if you have a very aggressive agent, he'll sell it to another studio."

In other cases, a studio will buy a script to keep it away from the competition. If, say, Universal is developing a project that is very similar to one on the market that the buyers are bidding on, Universal then outbids its competitors to take the script off the market and keep them from developing something similar.

The competitive mentality also exists within a studio, which may put two similar projects in development in hopes that one will emerge superior to the other and attract the best talent.

THE BUSINESS OF COMMERCIALITY

When you come right down to it, no one really knows what will be commercial. What sounds like a hot concept on paper may strike out at the box office. Look at FRIED GREEN TOMA-TOES. It isn't conceptually commercial by Hollywood standards, but proved so touching and had such strong performances that it became a commercial success.

"Something might not seem readily commercial because it's about WWII," says agent Mike Marcus. "But I think anything could be commercial if well enough done and not too esoteric."

So instead of thinking of commerciality as a negative, an attack on your creativity as a writer, think of it as big screen entertainment—the opportunity to write a movie that millions will see and enjoy. If you can take *that* kind of script to a studio, you're in.

If you're intensely passionate about it, all the better. If not, don't beat yourself over the head with the idea that a commercial script isn't worth pursuing because your heart's not really in it. If a million-plus deal falls in your lap—*take it!*

Says Susan Morgan Williams, vice-president of development for Percy Main Productions (director Ridley Scott's company), "Though I'm the last person to advise a writer to write something that is very contemporary and commercial, I would also say that it's the only way you're going to get in the door.

"If you have a marginally commercial script, maybe you'll find an agent and have somewhat of a calling card. But I would encourage every new writer to write a commercial script because if you're going to stick to the smaller, more personal stories, you're going to have a very long road ahead of you."

4

The Story

Let's cut to the chase. If a story doesn't ignite within the first 5 to 15 pages of a script, most executives, producers, and agents are going to stop reading and toss that script right into the reject pile.

Says production v.p. Michael Schulman, "The most important part of a script is probably the first 5 or 10 pages because, as sad as it is, you see a lot of executives coming home with 20 scripts a weekend. And if you're reading what you perceive as bad writing...a bad opening, or a script that doesn't move in those 5 or 10 pages...an executive isn't going to get much further than that.

"Within the first 10 pages I want something that I haven't seen before: either in the writing, or a situation, or a kind of intensity that breaks through the complacency that we all feel when we're sitting home with a stack of scripts to get through. Something that just shakes you up a little bit..."

"If I like what I'm reading right off the bat," says Gregory Avellone, vice-president of development for Kevin Costner's Tig Productions, "then I'm willing to be a little bit more open-minded about problems that might need to be worked on later in the script. But I generally find that writers don't make good use of the first ten or fifteen pages of a script, and those are the most crucial."

In other cases, you may not even have 5 pages to strut your stuff.

Says writer Matt Tabak, former vice-president of development for Silver Pictures, "I used to work for Don Simpson and Jerry Bruckheimer (producers of TOP GUN, BEVERLY HILLS COP, FLASHDANCE, DAYS OF THUNDER), who would put a script down *after a page*! A writer must realize that whoever is reading their script reads so many of them, day in and day out. They'll just put it down if they're not interested. So you've got to hook 'em. Hook 'em *fast*."

Good writers have a way of hooking you at the start, wasting no time in pulling you into the world of the story and enmeshing you in the lives of the characters. There's an intriguing setup, and a dilemma presents itself to the protagonist that makes you eager to learn what's going to happen next. But the truth is that many writers flat-out fail to make you care about anything that happens in the script, much less the first ten pages, and it often takes too long to understand what the story is about.

MAKE IT CLEAR EARLY ON WHAT THE STORY IS ABOUT

Says Universal's Leonard Kornberg, "I'll be 30 pages in and say, 'What the hell is this about? I do not know what this is about.' And if you can't tell what the hell the story is about, at least within the first act, the script is going to be a bail [pass]." The writer has failed to establish the central conflict, so I have no sense of what's going to pull me through the script. It's just kind of meandering and mushy for the first 25-30 pages and there's no central relationship, which is a serious problem.

"The writer needs to set up the central conflict as early as possible instead of getting caught up in empty, atmospheric scenes that don't mean anything. Once you establish what's going to pull the reader through, then you can be atmospheric because you've conveyed what the real core of the story is."

To be sure, the problem with many bad scripts is the languor with which the writer sets up the story. It doesn't kick in early;

the writer is going around in circles for the first 40, 50, 60 pages, conveying little or nothing of what the story is about. That kind of writing will not hook anybody. Guaranteed.

Explains agent Robert Stein of United Talent Agency, "I think the biggest problem that I have with scripts is that my attention isn't grasped quick enough. I find myself confused in that I don't know what the story is, who the characters are, what their motivation is."

Screenwriter Leslie Dixon is often asked to do rewrites, and what plagues many of the scripts she reads is a vague, protracted setup. "It takes forever to set up the premise," says Dixon. "I read scripts where I'm on page 47 and I still don't know what's going on. And then on page 52 I say, 'Oh, now I get it. This man who has come to earth from another world has to take a job as a rich man's cleaning lady and they're going to fall in love,' Now I'm making that up as kind of an awful sounding comedic premise, but the point is that the writer has taken until page 52 to get there, whereas he could have gotten there on page 17 and told me where this movie was going to go."

So in the writing of your story, *you must convey early on what it is. What is it about? Where is it going?* Kick that story in as soon as possible.

But even if your story kicks in early and is clearly presented, it may still be too bland to catch anyone's eye. You must therefore ask yourself: How can I make this story unique, imaginative, and exciting enough to hook and hold the reader from start to finish? How can I steer clear of what has been done a million times and really write a story that stands out? Because if you can do that and do it well, you're in business.

"I get excited when a writer comes up with something completely unique," says Meg Ryan's development head Cathy Rabin, "the kind of writer that makes me wonder: Where did this come from? How did she ever imagine this story and these characters? Whoever this writer is, I want to be in business with them. Truly good writing is rare and always appreciated."

Adds Robert Stein, "The most important thing I look for is a good story. Is it interesting and unique enough to take us somewhere that we haven't been before? Does it show us something we haven't seen before, or put a new light on something we have seen so we see it differently? That's what interests me."

Does your story do any of these things? Does it have the capacity to hook even the most jaded people in the business who have seen practically everything under the sun? Well, that's what your aim must be. So even if your script is in a stack of 20 that someone is taking home that weekend, your story should be so strong and fresh that the person can't help but say, "Wow. This is pretty damn good." But just what does it take to achieve that?

THE CENTRAL CONFLICT

The vital ingredient in any story is a compelling central conflict. It defines what your entire story is about.

Two women are on the run from the law after a rape and murder (THELMA & LOUISE). A radio talk show host is out to redeem himself after his comments trigger a murderous psychopath (THE FISHER KING). A woman comes to grips with the harsh realities of old age and being chauffeured about (DRIVING MISS DAISY).

The central conflict must be strong enough to sustain the story over the long haul. The problem with many scripts, however, is that the central conflict lacks substance, the story petering out around p. 60 as the writer strains to keep it alive.

Recently I read a script in which a monkey turns into a man, who still behaves like a monkey. Now while this is sort of cute and funny at first, the central conflict limits the writer in that there are just so many scenes you can have of the man eating bananas, swinging from chandeliers, screeching and making funny faces. The story is also limited by the fact that the man/monkey is in love with his female owner, but the romantic element of the story is undermined because the woman can't very well make love to her monkey. So there just isn't much room for the story to build and grow.

Another common problem, at least in the Hollywood mainstream, is a central conflict turn which the majority of moviegoers wouldn't likely find accessible or involving.

In selecting the central conflict of your story, you must ask yourself: Why do I care? Why would anybody care? Does the central conflict lay the foundation for a truly compelling story? Does it have the substance to really go the distance? Are the stakes high enough? Is it clear *early on* what the story is about? Is it enough of a departure from what has been done before? Does it have the potential to not only hook the reader, but captivate a healthy chunk of the moviegoing public?

It is imperative that the *stakes of the story* be high enough to sufficiently challenge and threaten the protagonist. Yet this is where many scripts go wrong. The protagonist doesn't stand to lose enough because the stakes are too low.

The writer must pose the questions: What will happen if the protagonist *doesn't* succeed? What are the consequences? If the stakes aren't high enough, the quest of the protagonist won't seem as critical to the audience and it's harder to become emotionally involved in the story. This goes for both comedy and drama.

If Dr. Frankenstein (Gene Wilder) doesn't bring the monster to life in YOUNG FRANKENSTEIN, he will deem himself an abject failure and his Herculean efforts will be for naught. And if he doesn't save the monster later in the story, it will be killed.

In FATAL ATTRACTION, if Dan (Michael Douglas) doesn't succeed in destroying Alex (Glenn Close), the vicious psychopath with whom he has had an extramarital fling, he will lose everything that is near and dear to him.

In BACK TO THE FUTURE, if Marty McFly (Michael J. Fox) doesn't get his mother and father together in the past, he and his entire family will fade away in the future. And if he doesn't drive through the electrical storm at just the precise moment, he will miss his chance to go back to the future and prevent his friend Doc from being killed by Libyan terrorists.

For producer Sarah Pillsbury (of Sanford/Pillsbury), the premise "must be some sort of moral, philosophical, political or psychological dilemma." Her picture RIVER'S EDGE, for example, the story of a murder among a group of teenagers, is "a study of the different kind of moral responses people have to any particular situation and their ability to act on those responses. Everybody in that script represents a different moral point of view. For instance, the character Matt must decide whether he will follow his conscience, which means going against his best friend and turning another friend in to the police—whom he mistrusts because he's a dope-smoking teenager. But he has the courage to do what he thinks is right. Clarissa, on the other hand, immediately has the appropriate moral response, but is unable to challenge the leadership of her peer group."

In another Sanford/Pillsbury film, DESPERATELY SEEKING SUSAN, the Rosanna Arquette character gets amnesia, forgets who she is, and by assuming another person's identity, discovers her own identity in the process.

You see? The more the protagonist stands to lose, the higher the stakes and the more compelling the story. If you have even an inkling that the premise is too slight and inconsequential, strengthen it or start from scratch. Don't wait for the powers that be to clue you in.

A STORY MUST BE EMOTIONALLY INVOLVING

A script will be rejected if it fails to strike an emotional chord. It doesn't make you laugh, cry, angry, happy...nothing. It's emotionally void. You don't care about the characters or become emotionally caught up in their world. The story merely grazes the surface and fails to engage you on a gut level. A scene is meant to be a tearjerker and you read it dry-eyed. A character is dying of a dreadful disease and you might as well be reading your grocery list. The script fails to hit you in the heart, nor does it have any... *PASS*.

On the other hand, heartfelt stories that grab you emotionally get all the praise they deserve.

On her initial read of THE LONG WALK HOME, the story of a middle-class white housewife and her black housekeeper in Alabama during the bus boycott of 1955 (starring Sissy Spacek and Whoopi Goldberg), Parkway v.p. Andrea Asimow "was moved so profoundly by this beautiful script. It had incredible honesty. People talked like somebody was home inside their heart and soul, as opposed to character types moving through the page saying what those character types might ordinarily say. And if I am so passionate about a piece of material, I won't stop pushing and talking about it."

Says Fandango Films' Cathy Rabin, "There are scripts that just seem to pack an extraordinary emotional wallop. They can be in any genre and about any topic, but something about them grabs you. I tend to dismiss stories that are emotionally void. I feel that at its core, a script is storytelling. And storytelling has been the same throughout the ages: it's about the human experience.

"I have a fondness for writers who get under the skin of the characters," Rabin continues, "allowing the audience to emotionally invest themselves in the story. If the writer forgets that or supplants that critical factor with devices (action, broad humor, special effects), it's inherently less interesting to me."

As such, always keep the emotional aspects of your story in mind. It is essential that you pull the reader into your story and give him or her something to care about, someone to feel for. Your story must have heart and a solid emotional center—even in a comedy—or it's near impossible to become involved.

A good example is ARTHUR, which was filled to the brim with laughs, yet contained strong emotional elements as well. The audience genuinely cared when the John Gielgud character, Arthur's friend and aide, died. It truly cared when Arthur fell in love with a waitress and had to choose between love and poverty, or wealth and loneliness.

This is one of the prime reasons why scripts are passed on: a dearth of emotional engagement. The writer has failed to delve beneath the surface. And if even the writer has no feeling for the material, how can anybody else?

But there is another side to this: some scripts are rejected for trying too hard to make you feel. They're excessively mawkish, sentimental, and melodramatic. The writer pulls every lever he can think of to hit you in the heart. Such stories end up eliciting the opposite response. Instead of becoming caught up in the story, the reader is too aware of the writer's machinations to feel anything. The plotting is syrupy and overwrought...*PASS*.

I've seen a *lot* of scripts tossed aside for this reason, and if you're a writer who's unable to decipher between genuine emotion and tear-stained goo, get some help before you show that script to anyone in a decision-making position.

A STORY MUST BE BELIEVABLE AND LOGICAL

A script is ripe for attack if it isn't sufficiently believable.

If the reader spends more time questioning the plausibility of the story than being entertained by it; if little or nothing rings true; if plot turns and character actions have a phony, contrived ring to them; if there isn't a logical progression of events or sufficient reasoning behind the actions of the characters...*PASS*.

The minute the reader stops believing, they're no longer involved in the story and the script is a shoo-in for rejection.

You must examine your story from all angles and *question everything before someone else does.* Is every plot turn real and believable? Are the actions of the characters adequately justified and sufficiently motivated? Is there the slightest chance that something doesn't ring true or doesn't make sense? In other words, don't leave *any holes* unplugged. The trained eye will spot these holes immediately and use them as ammunition to reject it.

However, it should be noted that there are times when a slight stretch of credibility and logic is acceptable given the nature of a story and the demands of a particular genre.

In the finale of JAGGED EDGE, for instance, defense attorney Teddy (Glenn Close) is alone in her house, in bed, at night, after discovering that her client Jack (Jeff Bridges) is indeed guilty of the murders for which he has just been acquitted. Such knowledge puts Teddy in grave danger, of which she is well aware, and the logical thing for her to do would be to get the hell out of there and call the police. But given the demands of the thriller genre (that the protagonist and killer must battle it out in the third act), screenwriter Joe Eszterhas realized this and had Teddy lying in wait for Jack, essentially waiting to kill or be killed. Jack has to come after Teddy and she has to be alone. To write it any other way would dilute the story.

Tension and suspense rise as Jack bursts into Teddy's house, the momentum building to the breaking point as she finally shoots him dead. Although one could question why Teddy is alone in the house at all, knowing she's a target, had she been safely tucked away somewhere or had called the police, there would be no story.

Another example: In HOME ALONE, had Kevin (Macaulay Culkin) called 911 at the first sight of the burglars, there would be no movie. But because it's a larger-than-life comedy, with elements of fantasy, and because the story's entire reason for being is having the boy ingeniously outwit the burglars with one devilish trap after another, what may seem rather unbelievable becomes vastly entertaining within the context of this particular story. Produced for $18 million, HOME ALONE made ten times that amount domestically in its first three months of release.

In your writing, then, you must achieve a balance between plausibility and entertainment. You must plug the gaping holes and gaps in character motivation that drastically undermine the credibility of your story, yet be able to stretch credibility ever so slightly, given the demands of a particular story and genre. It's a thin line to walk.

When you're faced with this dilemma and don't know quite how to proceed, watch a well-crafted film which successfully avoids the problems you're trying to overcome in your script. I'll often put such suggestions in my comments, advising the writer of a poorly executed thriller to watch FATAL ATTRACTION or the French classic LES DIABOLIQUES. It always helps to examine what works and then apply it to your writing.

THE WORLD OF YOUR STORY

When you like a movie enough to see it two, three, four, five, maybe six times, it is often because you can't wait to be pulled back into *the world of the story*—its setting, milieu. Whether it's a spaceship, baseball field, TV news office, or a summer resort in the Catskills, there is something about a carefully constructed, well-delineated world in a motion picture that makes you want to return to it again and again and again.

"A richly created world on the page will attract my attention, " says Parkway Productions' Andrea Asimow. "I am very attracted to being transported from a familiar world that I live in. And if the writer is effective in creating that world for me, then I lose myself, have a wonderful experience, and feel enriched by it. I feel as if I've taken a little vacation from my own reality and I really love that."

Amblin's Jason Hoffs says, "If a writer can bring us into a totally new, exciting, vibrant world that we haven't seen or felt before, that's terrific. It's very hard for me to remember the last time anybody did that in a spec script."

"One thing that I really favor when I read scripts," says Geoffery Grode, a story analyst for 20th Century Fox, "is when the writer takes me into a new and different world. I particularly liked THE BIG EASY because it was set in New Orleans and not in New York or L.A.—locations that have been done to death."

So there is a definite awareness in the business of the milieu of a story, and its careful selection by the writer can create excitement or boredom.

If the characters are strong enough, the story can simply take place in a room and be thoroughly involving—as in John Hughes' THE BREAKFAST CLUB, about a group of high school students thrown together in detention.

But some stories are more dependent on setting than others, and many scripts aren't worth pursuing precisely because the world of the story is too mundane.

To illustrate, I read a script which bore a strong resemblance to the plot of the classic film ALL ABOUT EVE, in which stage star Margo Channing (Bette Davis) is cunningly usurped by Eve Harrington, a conniving young actress she takes under her wing. But while that film takes place in the dazzling world of the Broadway theater, the script I read detracts from the story by setting it in the dull milieu of a Cleveland restaurant. The Margo

81

Channing character is a restaurateur, and you just don't care enough that the woman she hires as manager sets out to take over the restaurant. No matter how fiercely ambitious she is, the ruthless climb of a restaurant manager somehow lacks the intensity the story demands. As a result, the script was passed on.

On the other hand, there was a television movie starring Barbara Eden and Heather Locklear as journalists covering the political beat in Washington. It, too, bore a similarity to ALL ABOUT EVE (Eden being a journalistic star and Locklear the ambitious young neophyte craving for power), but the world of the story created the necessary drama and excitement. Most people are intrigued by the goings-on in Washington, and the lives of political journalists prove exceedingly more watchable than those of restaurant professionals in Ohio.

So you must consider whether your story demands a thrilling milieu, or can withstand the ordinary.

But don't stop there. You must then create a specific set of parameters for that world, both through imagination and—when called for—research.

YOU MUST KNOW THE WORLD OF YOUR STORY

Before writing BROADCAST NEWS, James Brooks painstakingly researched the world of broadcast journalism. He spent time in newsrooms, interviewed journalists—anything he could to soak up the atmosphere and learn the inner workings of that world. In doing so, Brooks was able to create an authentic, detailed setting instead of merely skimming the surface and glazing over the specifics.

"If you're not writing from your own personal experience," says writer Frank Pierson, "then you must thoroughly research your story." But as Pierson points out, many writers don't bother to do the necessary legwork to become fully versed in the world of their story. "It's like they have seen a thousand TV movies and are just following that formula—not bothering to get out on the street and spend some time with cops, if they're writing a cop movie, or writing a gang movie without even meeting a gang member. They go and read the newspapers about gangs and think they can get inside a gang member's head. You can't do that. Those scripts don't read like anybody knows anything about what they're writing...merely imitating what they've seen before."

For a story that probes into a specific world, such as stand-up comedy in PUNCHLINE, the financial world in WALL STREET, naval aviation in TOP GUN, the criminal justice system in PRESUMED INNOCENT, research becomes absolutely essential for the writer. For with knowledge you write with authority, and with that comes authenticity.

The writer must ask: How does this world operate? What are the rules? Who makes the rules? How do people behave? What are the particulars of this world and what makes it distinct? In other words: How can I avoid cliches?

Take, for example, a family drama set in a suburban home in the Midwest. How are you going to write it and avoid an overly familiar world filled with obvious conventions and predictable stereotypes? Is mom just another typical homemaker without a unique set of problems? Is dad a cardboard cut-out of a boozing construction foreman with a mean temper? Is the son a cliched replica of every angst-ridden teen who starts smoking pot? Does his college-age sister lack identifiable traits which are uniquely her own? If so, who cares?

If the writer is from L.A. and he doesn't visit the Midwest to soak up the atmosphere and observe people's behavior; if he doesn't spend time with a real Midwestern family to assess their values and sensibilities; if his writing amounts to guesswork, resulting in an ill-defined world inhabited by empty characters— that's how scripts get passed on.

Good writers, however, are constantly aware if what they're writing is vivid, real, and has a definitive edge. If it's a cop story, they not only walk the beat with the cops, but then look for ways to bend that information and make it unique.

Says story analyst Geoffery Grode, "The writer has to do everything possible to elevate the world of the story out of the stranglehold of cliches."

Even in the case of fantasy worlds, not only must they be enormously inventive and captivating, as in STAR WARS, but not so far afield from human experience that they preclude audience involvement.

In many poorly realized fantasy scripts, the writer is so caught up in creating a fantasy world of phantasmic proportions that the human element is virtually nonexistent. As a result, we get turned off. Particularly if what inhabits that world is primarily nonhuman, it becomes that much more important to infuse the characters and story with enough human emotion to hit us in the heart. You can dream up the most imaginative world that anyone has ever seen, but if everything else is devoid of the "stuff" that people care about, you're headed for rejection.

WHAT DOES YOUR STORY SAY?

Hollywood is big on stories with themes—stories that make a statement about society, the struggle of mankind, love, greed...something about the world in which we live. In fact, a common thread among buyers I've spoken with is that a story should not only make us think, but alter our perception.

Says Andrea Asimow, "I like stories that change, even if it's ever so slightly, the way an audience looks at something. I believe in films which release an audience into the streets, and have them thinking about something they've not quite thought about in that way before."

"I don't want intellectual and spiritual puzzles," says Mark Valenti, story analyst for Imagine Films Entertainment. "I want a story. If the writer does his job, I will be forced to think about life in a new way."

While Steven Reuther acknowledges that "some movies appear to be pure spectacle and fun, with no real theme," he tends to ask of scripts, "Is there some lesson to be learned that's of value, either by the characters or the telling of the story? Does it pose a question that is interesting and contemporary?"

Queries Sarah Pillsbury, "If it's a cop movie, what is it saying about criminal justice and First Amendment rights? If it's about politics, does the political message support the status quo or go against it? What vision does it present of society?"

Is it, as in SOUL MAN, that it's easier to get a scholarship to Harvard Law School if he impersonates a black? Is it, as in REVERSAL OF FORTUNE, that the rich and crafty get away with murder and can buy the best defense? Does love triumph in the end, as in CROSSING DELANCEY, or is it a heartbreaker as in THE WAY WE WERE?

What is your script saying? Does it say anything? Is there anything of value to be gained from the story?

Such questions are critical to Andrea Asimow: "At this company, when we like a script but we're a little on the fence about it, we ask: What is this script telling us? And is it important enough to spend two years putting it on the screen?

"Each and every script we contemplate, for the most part, we ask: What do we want the audience to get up from the theater and walk out in the street feeling or thinking? And we have to be able to name it. We have to be able to say it."

In the writing of your script, then, crystallize in your mind what you want to impart to the audience, and then think in terms of establishing a central argument or theme that you either prove or disprove through the course of the story.

In WHEN HARRY MET SALLY..., for instance, the central argument put forth by Billy Crystal's character in the first act is that men and woman are incapable of having a purely platonic relationship. Though Meg Ryan's character staunchly disagrees at first and is out to prove him wrong, she ultimately falls in love and, in proving him right, solidifies the premise of that particular film.

In THE DOCTOR, the argument is that doctors should empathize with and nurture their patients instead of treating them like slabs of meat. This is ultimately demonstrated when William Hurt, initially a cold, uncaring physician, contracts cancer and is treated with the same indifference as he administers to his own patients. It is through his moving bout with cancer that the film makes a powerful statement on doctor-patient relationships.

In BROADCAST NEWS, the argument is style vs. substance in the world of TV journalism. Journalist Aaron (Albert Brooks) is initially under the assumption that smarts and hard work will take him far, until anchor Tom (William Hurt) comes along to disprove that. Handsome and charming in front of a camera but admittedly uninformed (he doesn't even understand the news he's reading), Tom is soon on a fast track to success while Aaron is passed over. When he finally gets his big chance to anchor the news, he is coached by Tom not on substance but on style: sitting on his coat to keep the shoulders straight, punching certain words in his delivery and essentially "selling" the news. And though both Aaron and Jane are vehemently against such a theatrical form of broadcast journalism, the film ultimately says that style does win over substance, and it is precisely Tom's approach (feigning tears while interviewing a victim of date rape) that pushes him all the way to the top.

These films are centered around thought-provoking arguments or themes and definitely do cause you to view the world a bit differently—or at least feel compelled to question it. Can members of the opposite sex really just be friends? Should doctors have any connection to their patients beyond curing them? How much of what we see on the news is real and how much is phony? Are TV news anchors actually manipulating the news to hook the viewers?

Be just as probing about your own story. Ask whether the central argument or theme offers something to be gained, learned, thought about or discussed.

The central argument or theme should resonate throughout your entire story, not just a few scenes here and there. Each movement of a well-told story is centered around that argument, continually questioning and probing it from both sides.

Says story analyst Geofferey Grode, "You can make an argument that every movie is about something, but that is not the same as saying that the person who wrote it had this vast overview of what he was doing and tailored the entire script to develop that theme. That's what I find lacking in an incredible number of scripts."

Says writer Gary Ross, "The theme is the engine of story-telling, and it should intrinsically and organically ask an important question. The theme has to be an area that embodies intrinsic conflict that allows me to express what I'm trying to say. In BIG that would be the dilemma of growing up—the tugs we have toward where we're going versus where we've been. But many writers today write from a mechanical place, not because they want to say or express something. They don't realize that theme is the reason you're doing it, what you're trying to express."

Moreover, be careful in developing your theme that it's not expressed in heavy-handed symbolism, or simply blurted out by your characters. Don't scream out to the audience: Hey! This is my message! This is my theme! The minute something sounds too preachy and forced, it's wrong.

"We are in the entertainment business," says producer Howard Rosenman," and if you preach or are didactic, forget it. Sometimes people are skilful enough to weave into their films the messages they want to carry out. But if you don't entertain, forget it."

CROSSING OVER THE LINE: RACISM, SEXISM, BAD TASTE

Be aware that everyone in the business has their own set of sensibilities when assessing material. If a script crosses too far over the line from their perspective, it will be rejected.

Producer Lauren Shuler-Donner (RADIO FLYER, PRETTY IN PINK, ST. ELMO'S FIRE, LADYHAWKE, MR. MOM) says "There are certain stories that are too violent that I will not do. I will not do anything that has violence against women unless it's there to prove a point. For instance, the woman in RADIO FLYER is a victim of verbal abuse, but it's to prove a point that this is wrong. I won't show rape on the screen. I think that if one lunatic watches it and gets off on it then I'm doing a public disservice, so I refuse to do that."

"There are some lines I will not cross," says Andrea Asimow. "For instance, I would not promote a script that is a post-nuclear apocalyptic story, because I don't believe in putting forth images of a society surviving nuclear warfare. I feel it promotes the notion that we can survive something as cataclysmic as that, and therefore don't have to be as vigilant about preventing that kind of thing from happening.

"I was associate producer of a [nuclear-themed] film called TESTAMENT, but that was about the end of the world. What was so beautiful about that film was that we mourned the loss of the world as we knew it. People left that film grief-stricken, as opposed to films which say look at this wonderfully hip, bizarre world we could be living in after nuclear war.

"Other lines I won't cross have to do with roles of women in which they're being served up as objects with a lot of gratuitous sex and violence. I have turned down a lot of scripts that I think audiences would flock to, but they're anathema to me. And I'm lucky to be in a position to make that decision, a lot of times before the script ever gets to the next step."

So be aware if your story espouses morally reprehensible, blatantly sexist or racist behavior or may be exceedingly offensive to a particular race or class of people.

Granted, some religious groups attacked as blasphemous THE LAST TEMPTATION OF CHRIST, yet it was still released. BASIC INSTINCT took a lot of flap from gay and lesbian groups, but has emerged as the most successful R-rated film in history to date.

Yet in today's political, racial, and sexual climate, film executives are definitely concerned with the societal impact of a film and how it will be interpreted. Due to racial tensions resulting from the L.A. riots, for example, the title of Universal Pictures' LOOTERS (directed by Walter Hill) has been changed to TRESPASS. The film, centering on a pair of white firemen vs. two black crime lords in East St. Louis, has been temporarily yanked from Universal's release schedule.

Says Universal executive Leonard Kornberg, "I think the industry is beginning to be more conscious of violence in films.

I think there is a certain sense of responsibility on the part of the studios and filmmakers. In fact, everyone on the lot recently attended a meeting for James Brady's group on gun control and the Brady Bill."

Though violence is certainly prevalent in many films today, some stories are so over-the-top that they're more disgusting, unsavory and tasteless than viable pieces of entertainment. In my work as a story analyst, I've read scripts that conveyed ethnic or racial minorities as nothing but killers, rapists, and scumbags; or women as bimbo-headed sperm banks who should be beaten to a pulp and live under a man's rule. In a script I read recently, the message is that it's OK to kill animals for sport or watch them kill each other in a ring. None of these sort of scripts have, or will, get past me.

Another script comes to mind I read recently in which 98% of the story is an old man fending off a pack of wild bobcats. Not only does this come off as a gross exploitation of animals and a lame excuse for violence, but can you imagine the marketing for that picture? SEE AN OLD MAN GETTING ATTACKED BY BOBCATS! Needless to say, the script was a PASS.

Pay attention to what you are depicting and espousing in your story. Yes, you can always take your script to one of those companies that make exploitation films like "Killer Bimbos From Hell" and "Bambi The Preppy Prostitute," but if you're targeting the major studios and prominent production companies, you're better off not giving them what can be easily interpreted as overtly offensive, degrading, tasteless and vulgar.

DARK & DEPRESSING

A story may also be too dark and depressing for the Hollywood mainstream. Case in point: IRONWEED. Even with Meryl Streep and Jack Nicholson in starring roles, the film proved too dark and bleak to strike a chord with general moviegoers.

Granted, if Streep and Nicholson want to do your movie, no matter if it's the darkest, most depressing story in the world, that movie is going to get made. But without such star attachments going in, you're better off writing a script that doesn't cause the reader to want to jump off the nearest building.

While this in no way implies that every story must be happy-go-lucky and Pollyanna sweet, the major studios and production companies are far more interested in mass audience, commercial fare than some dark, arty little movie about suicide that takes place in a blackened sewer. That's a film better suited to the art house circuit, and if that isn't your target, then you're encouraged to write a script which is more accessible to "Middle America" than members of the Sylvia Plath fan club.

This also goes for the ending of your story. With very few exceptions, Hollywood films have upbeat endings. True, the husband and wife in THE WAR OF THE ROSES die in the end, but then the movie is a black comedy and the ending works within the context. But studio executives generally want movies to end 'up', or at least leave the audience with something that is positive.

Says Leonard Kornberg, "I worked with a writer whose script had a really, really depressing ending, but I felt that if not optimism, there should at least be some sense of hope. Because why is somebody going to want to experience some nihilistic depression? Almost no one will want to see that, and studios will never make a film with a horribly downbeat ending. Don't end your story with the main character sitting on a ledge, bleeding and staring out into space. Not that an ending should be stupidly happy, but it shouldn't be horribly depressing either."

SUBTEXT

There's an old adage that if the scene is about what the scene is about, it's dead. Or if two characters say "I love you" and mean it, the scene is over. In other words, a story must have *subtext*.

Subtext is what lies *beneath* the text. It can be the underlying meaning of a story, the subconscious motives of a character, or what is *really* going on moment by moment in a scene.

In the film STAND BY ME, the text of the story is that the boys are in search of a dead body. The subtext is their quest for maturity. In DANGEROUS LIAISONS, confessions of love are marked by underlying treachery and deceit. Says producer Sarah Pillsbury of RIVER'S EDGE, "What the movie is ultimately about is not there in the text. You can say that what's driving it along is that a murder has been committed, we know who the killer is, and we wonder if he'll get caught or do it again. But what the movie is really about is the difficulty of making moral choices in society."

Says producer Howard Rosenman, "Subtext drives character, and the character's underlying flaw is the subtext which becomes the spine of the movie. In CASABLANCA, for example, Bogart's underlying flaw is that he couldn't commit, and all the actions of the scenes are about that lack of commitment. When it finally comes down to a choice between love and duty, he was able to overcome his flaw of commitment by doing what is best for the woman he loves and also commit to the political cause."

"THELMA & LOUISE," says development v.p. Susan Morgan Williams, "is typical of what we look for as far as subtext. The story has this veneer of action-adventure, but underneath there's this very strong subtext which is about freedom, rape of women and why society doesn't treat it very well."

The audience senses the subtext as a story unfolds. Like the theme, it should in no way be blatantly announced by the characters. It would have been extremely heavy-handed, for example, if Thelma and Louise conveyed in words to the audience, "You know, we're so much freer now than before. Our journey epitomizes freedom, and what we're fighting against has so much meaning and validity."

It sounds laughable when you say it that way, but that's what bad writers do. They flatly announce everything to the audience instead of allowing the subtext to naturally flow from the *actions* of the characters.

Often characters will have both conscious and unconscious goals as they progress through the story, the latter serving as the subtext of their quest. A character may not be aware that he wants something other than what he is actively pursuing, but the audience becomes aware of it and can identify with it.

Often the conscious and unconscious goals are in opposition to one other—a man committing a series of murders, when what he's really doing is crying out in pain and loneliness; a woman shutting herself off from the world, when what she really wants is to be loved. Such dichotomies enhance and create complexity in a character. Something is brewing beneath the surface.

The same applies to writing a scene. If it's too flat and on-the-nose, the person reading the script will immediately be turned off. If you're writing a scene in which two people can't wait to throw each other to the floor and make love, the most obvious thing in the world is to have them say just that. Better to have them engaged in some form of action or behavior that has absolutely nothing to do with romance, yet the subtext beneath the dialogue tells you that these two characters are hot for each other.

Don't forget that actors are acutely conscious of subtext. As a writer, be aware that they can often say more with a look, touch, or other piece of behavior than words ever could.

"Leave room for the actors to emote," advises producer Ed Feldman. "Most people overwrite because they don't think that anyone understands what they're saying. But less is always more. The stars tell you the plot with their eyes."

Adds screenwriter Larry Ferguson, "Motivation can be conveyed by actors that isn't on the page, and the actual filming of an experience can be much more specific than the writing. What a writer thinks may be vague or missing in a script could be conveyed on screen."

So resist the urge to overwrite. If you feel compelled to explain the underlying root of a scene or motivations of the characters, *do not* put it in dialogue. Off-camera directions—as long as they're not needlessly wordy—can aid the reader in grasping the subtext of your story.

TONE

Before you begin writing, establish in your own mind the tone of your story. Be specific. Is it quirky? Dark? Surreal? Satiric? Once you establish that, calculate whether the tone will markedly shift at some point or if you intend to sustain it throughout. If the latter is your aim, be consistent. Otherwise, make sure that the changes in tone aren't so drastic and awkward that they aren't organic to the story. Avoid a strangely comic moment in a drama, or a broad, acerbic satire which steadily softens in tone until the satire disappears altogether.

In reading the coverage of other story analysts, I've often seen scripts attacked for being tonally inconsistent. The analyst will say something like, "It begins as a slapstick comedy, but then shifts to black comedy and drama, the writer unable to sustain an even tone throughout."

Other problems occur when the tone of a *subplot* (a secondary or subordinate plot) is drastically inconsistent with that of the main plot. Explains Paramount story analyst Norm Saulnier, "I'll be reading a script that suddenly goes off on a weird tangent that's different in tone to the rest of the story. For instance, if a writer is breezing along with a nice, fluffy character comedy and then goes off on a dark, depressing subplot—something so out of left field that it it's a complete tonal departure from the rest of the story—that's a problem."

When skillfully written, however, tonal shifts aren't strikes against a story. They enhance it.

If you recall the Jonathan Demme film SOMETHING WILD, it begins as a funny road comedy between Melanie Griffith and Jeff Daniels, and then turns dark and sinister about midway through with the entrance of the villain, Ray Liotta. But it works. The transition is smooth and exciting, steering the story down an unexpected path as the audience is thrown for a loop.

A major tonal shift is also found in TERMS OF ENDEAR-MENT, which contains some hilarious moments in the first half, then becomes a tearjerker in the second as Debra Winger's character withers away from cancer and dies. But instead of being an awkward tonal shift, the story becomes undeniably poignant and it's doubtful that anyone, unless they were made of stone, left the theater after that movie without crying their eyes out.

Certainly a zany comedy can tolerate moments of tenderness and romance, a drama, moments of comic relief. But there's a big difference between carefully orchestrated tonal shifts within a story and a slapdash compilation of tonal incongruities. Examine your script for such weaknesses, and always question whether shifts in tone will enhance your story or cause the reader to cite them as narrative flaws.

TIMELINESS

The word "fresh" comes up over and over again in my discussions with the buyers. They want stories that offer something for today's audiences and will reject anything that feels hackneyed and dated.

Sometimes I'll read a script and it just feels shopworn, as if it has been floating around for years. Other times you know for certain it's been floating around for years because the writer hasn't bothered to take off the date on the title page and has left telltale signs in the dialogue. For instance, the story is supposedly set in the present, yet a line reads, "Hey, get with the times, Billy! It's 1982!" *Writers: these are dead giveaways that your script has long been on the market and still hasn't sold!*

In other cases, the values or actions of the characters don't seem in tune to contemporary society. Or the script may plug into a trend that has long since passed. Or the central issues are no longer timely. It all seems rather old and tired.

Good writers take care to see that this doesn't happen. Lowell Ganz, with partner Babaloo Mandel, has written such hits as SPLASH, CITY SLICKERS, NIGHT SHIFT, and A LEAGUE OF THEIR OWN. Although LEAGUE is set in 1943, Ganz and Mandel were aware of writing the script for a contemporary audience. "The style is in the time in which it was depicted," says Ganz, "but the sensibilities are modern in that we're looking at that time period through this end of the telescope. The sexism that exists in the film is totally accurate for the time, but it's constructed in such a way that we're aware that today's audience is watching it."

So if you're writing a period story, be aware of making it palatable for today's moviegoer. And if your story is set in the present but was written ten years ago, don't assume that no one will note the dated references. *They will.* As such, delete the date from the title page, and make the necessary changes.

LOSING CONTROL: THE REALITIES OF SELLING A STORY

If you manage to sell a script to a studio, odds are that you won't have a hand in its development. After that, if by some miracle you're kept on the project throughout, consider yourself lucky—very lucky.

Says Universal's Leonard Kornberg, "What happens typically is that the original writer contractually gets two official 'paid passes' at the script: a first draft and a set of revisions [a draft and a set]. The set comes after the executive has given the writer notes [feedback and suggested changes] from the first draft. Then once the contractual obligations have been met, the studio has the option to replace the writer."

What's more, once a project becomes studio property, the original writer usually relinquishes all creative control.

Scott Alexander, writer with Larry Karaszewski of PROBLEM CHILD and its sequel, told me their original pitch was not a zany kid's movie but more of a black comedy from an adult perspective. But after selling the idea to Universal and turning in the first draft, the writers found that the studio wanted to take the project in a different direction and they were replaced. And while the team was brought back late in the game to do some rewriting, the point is that what ultimately became the story for PROBLEM CHILD was a far cry from the writers' original vision and they had no control over the changes. The picture became a big success and the team was hired to write the sequel, but even though they were given more creative control this time around, they still had to base their script on a movie they had initially conceived but only remotely resembled their original story.

"Most writers have very little say in script changes," says producer Ed Feldman. "The larger the amount of money involved, the less writers have a say. I've never met a director who takes a script and says, 'This is perfect, let's make it.' And when the director is finally satisfied with the script, you have to get some big star to be in it. Before you know it, the script has been changed drastically again."

This displeases many writers, but it's just the nature of the business.

"Most screenwriters I know are not happy people because they've been bludgeoned, cut apart," says novelist Warren Adler. "The writer is the lowest form of animal in Hollywood. If I needed the money and was desperate as a writer in this town, I think I would be unhappy 24 hours a day. Everyone gets accommodated but the writer."

"You're a tailor, creating a suit to custom-fit a star or director," says writer Richard Price. "When we [Price and director Martin Scorsese] were working on THE COLOR OF MONEY, we'd show Paul Newman something we liked, but if Paul didn't like it, we rewrote it to Paul's vision of himself as an actor. What you end up realizing is that whatever doesn't kill you makes you stronger." (*The Hollywood Reporter* 6/4/92)

Such is the writer's dilemma. You work your tail off and finally sell something, only to have other people dictate what the final screen version of your script will be.

There is one solution: Write *and* direct. This is the route taken by James Toback, who's directed every movie made from his screenplays except THE GAMBLER and BUGSY.

"Anyone who sells a script to a studio" says Toback, "and then says I expect this movie to be done my way, is living on a level of such naivete that it's hard to believe that what that person writes could have any kind of awareness or sense of how the world works. If you're selling your script to a corporation, you have to assume there's a good chance that the story will be turned into something unrecognizable. The easiest way to maintain control is to direct the movie yourself. You ultimately have to pay to keep control, but if you care about your work, that's what you do."

On the other side of the control issue are the executives.

"I resent when they resent the process," says New Regency president Steven Reuther. "I think if writers want no input they should do readings at their own house. The writer isn't always right, and collaboration is by definition what moviemaking is.

"You hire a star and a star director, and what are you going to tell them? That their ideas aren't good because they're not the same as the writer had? That's sort of a silly conversation. If a certain speech or notion in a screenplay is something that the director or an actor violently opposes, they're not going to do it very well and you're not serving the movie."

SCREEN CREDIT

The issue of screen credit is another sore subject for many screenwriters, particularly when you do major rewrites on a script and the original writer is the only one credited when the movie is released.

When many writers individually contribute to a screenplay, which is quite often the case, the decision of who gets credit may go to the Writers Guild arbitration committee, which then reads all the drafts to see who has made the most significant contribution "to the shooting script."

According to the Writers Guild Screen Credits Manual, "Any writer whose work represents a contribution of more than 33% of a screenplay shall be entitled to screenplay credit, except where the screenplay is an original screenplay. In the case of an original screenplay, any subsequent writer or writing team must contribute 50% to the final screenplay." [Note: "original" meaning not adapted from or based on material from another medium.]

Such rules are in place to protect the original writer, and yet a subsequent writer can change all of the dialogue and still not get credit. According to the manual, "There have been instances in which every line has been changed and still the Committee can find no significant change in the screenplay as a whole. There have been instances in which a change in one portion of the script is so significant that the entire screenplay is affected by it, and credit is awarded even though on a numerical count of lines and pages the writer may not qualify."

Says one prominent writer, who requests anonymity, such rules can be very disconcerting—to say the least.

"At least 50-60% of all writer screen credits are totally inaccurate. It can be very hard for a writer to get screen credit, even if they've written most of the movie. There are writers who have been nominated for "Best Screenplay" Oscars, and I know for a fact that most of the work was done by other writers. And yet the writer will get up there and thank the Academy like they wrote the whole thing.

"The way the Guild decides credits is based on what writer has contributed the most to the story. 'Written by' means story, whereas the dialogue means nothing. I have written almost every line of dialogue in a movie, but because I didn't change the story, I didn't get credit."

So by the time a movie hits the screen and one writer is credited, who knows how many writers actually played a hand in the script at one time or another?

Writer Nicholas Meyer, for example, did some uncredited rewriting on FATAL ATTRACTION and Paramount's upcoming thriller THE TEMP. Leslie Dixon did some uncredited work on Touchstone's BIG BUSINESS. Robert Towne's uncredited "script doctoring" is known to include FATAL ATTRACTION, FRANTIC, EIGHT MILLION WAYS TO DIE, REDS, THE GODFATHER, and BONNIE AND CLYDE (*Film Comment*, Nov-Dec. 1990). And Elaine May, one of the most coveted script doctors in the business, is known to have worked on TOOTSIE.

Some high-priced writers may choose not to be credited on a film for a variety of reasons, particularly when a film doesn't seem destined for box office glory. Due to a lack of creative control once the shooting starts (a film is the director's baby by then), a writer may have their names removed from the credits altogether, or use a pseudonym.

Writer Ed Naha (co-writer of HONEY, I SHRUNK THE KIDS), for example, used the pseudonym M. Kane Jeeves in the credits of the film CHUD II. A pseudonymous "Rob Morton" was credited with writing SWING SHIFT, after such heavyweights as Robert Towne and Bo Goldman took their names off. Phil Alden Robinson (FIELD OF DREAMS, co-writer of SNEAKERS) was credited as Jack T.D. Robinson on the less than memorable RELENTLESS. (*Variety,* 3/21/90)

But in the end...

GOOD STORYTELLING IS WHAT IT'S ALL ABOUT

The bottom line is that when we in the business read scripts, what we're essentially looking for is *a good story, well told.* Yes, characters are absolutely an integral part of the mix, and there are some who place characters above all else (see Chapter 6). But if the story is riddled with weaknesses, has nothing to say, if it has no direction and fails to ignite, the characters will be wandering around aimlessly and who will care about them.

I have rejected many a script because there was simply *NO STORY.* And while you may be a writer who's just called in for dialogue and character polishes, the ability to tell a crackling good story is no doubt a strong asset in any writer's arsenal.

As summed up by agent Lee Rosenberg: "Some people are good storytellers instinctually, like a camp counselor sitting around a campfire, mesmerizing a group of kids. That's what writers are. We're all sitting around the campfire waiting for the writer to tell us a good story."

A RECAP

—You can't afford to waste a second of time launching your story in the freshest, most captivating way imaginable

—It must be clear early on what your story is about

—You must create a compelling central conflict

—Your story must be emotionally involving

—Your story must be believable and logical

—You must be pulled into the world of the story—a world that is interesting, authentic, and definitely not cliched

—Your story must have a theme

—Ultimately, what does your story say? What view of the world is it conveying to the audience? Is it thought-provoking, hopeful, depressing, sexist, racist, morally reprehensible?

—Your story should have subtext

—Is your story tonally consistent?

—Is your story tired and dated, failing to offer enough for today's audiences? Are there dead giveaways within the story that the script was written years ago and still hasn't sold?

—Writers typically have little or no control once their script has been sold, and may not be credited on a film to which they have contributed.

5

Structure

The building of a successful screenplay is inextricably linked to its structure—the construction of a story from the ground up. How does it begin? Where does it go? How does it move? Does it build or sag? Is there sufficient conflict? Is the scene progression too talky and linear? Does the script fall apart during the second act? Is the ending weak?

Failure of the beginning or struggling writer to consider such critical questions pertaining to structure is like issuing your script a death warrant. While some of the top writers in the business claim to just improvise their way through a script without even thinking about structure, they can afford to take that approach because they know what they're doing and their skills have been proven. "We're all improvisational," says writer Darryl Ponicsan, "but I can assure you that the good writers know where they're going."

As such, the importance of a solid narrative structure cannot be overstated in this fiercely competitive business. Don't try to wing it if you don't know what you're doing; it will show on the page. Don't kid yourself that you know proper screenplay construction, only to meet with an executive who had a hell of a time getting through your script. Even if your story contains some intriguing, workable elements, you can't bank on that being reason enough to launch your script into development.

Explains Cathy Rabin, "We always seem to be weighing a script's strengths against its liabilities, and as we go through that process, we need to determine whether the shortcomings are readily fixable, or so mired that once you start plowing through a rewrite, the entire plot will fall apart and you'll be left starting from square one. The bottom line seems to be that a script can be well written and the story unsuitable, but the story can never be poorly written and worthy of consideration."

That hopefully sends a strong message to the writers whose screenplays typically read like this: after a lightweight opening brimming with pace-deadening dialogue, the story finally kicks in around page 55. But because he lacks the skill to keep building from there, what ensues is a flat, seemingly directionless series of scenes without sufficient conflict, urgency, excitement, momentum, tension, suspense—anything that keeps the story moving forward and sustains the reader's interest. The progressive complications resemble a string of loosely-linked vignettes. The ending is either maddeningly predictable or lacks a definite closure, leaving a host of unanswered questions in its wake. The result: *PASS*.

Sound familiar? If so, read on.

A script is typically a PASS for Paramount Pictures story analyst Norm Saulnier if "there's not a lot of development to it. The writer doesn't set up the characters, the pace is sluggish, there's no point to the story, the characters don't go anyplace." He also views with disfavor "stories that take too long to get going. The first act setup lasts 50 or 60 pages."

Executive Steven Reuther takes a negative view of a script that is "fraught with holes, is ambiguous in its resolution and the characters aren't figured out." He also believes that "A script shouldn't be too long or too short. It should be a movie, it should be professional. It should be something I can make that's under two hours and over an hour-and-a-half."

Indeed, those who evaluate and purchase screenplays generally take a dim view of those which are excessive in length. Couldn't the writer trim the fat out of his script? Can't he tell that there are perhaps 60 to 80 pages that are nothing but filler? Granted, length becomes a non-issue if the script is great, and James Toback says he doesn't even worry about how many pages his scripts are going to be. But then Toback is a pro. For those, however, who are cranking out long-winded, mediocre scripts, their prospects are dubious.

But all is not lost. Because structure can be learned, and we're about to trudge into the thick of it.

THE THREE-ACT STRUCTURE

When referring to screenplay structure in Hollywood, we're generally talking about first act, second, act, third act—beginning, middle, end. There's a definite launch in the first act, a solid confrontation in the second, and a resolution in the third. Though some European and art films may use experimental or anti-structure stories, and often do, "In Hollywood," says producer Howard Rosenman, "You follow the form."

"I am very conscious of the three-act structure," says executive Michael Schulman. "It's something that's talked about when I have development meetings. It just helps the process of writing and rewriting if you can break the script into three distinct units and say, 'This is where we need to be at the end of act one, this is what act two is about' and so on."

"The fact that writing is a form of communication necessitates being aware of structure," says writer Tom Schulman, "because you're basically telling a story, and stories have beginnings, middles and ends. They have to grab you early, interest you in the middle, and move you at the end. That structure is at work whenever we tell a story of any length, in any form. So those things are only there to help you. Where they hurt is when you get mechanical about them and try to invent things which are external to the internal logic of the story."

103

We'll be examining such weaknesses in this chapter and tackling structure from all angles. Bear in mind, however, that you should only view the following as a guide, not a list of rules that can't be broken. You don't want to become so mechanized in your writing that it suffers creatively.

Certain books on craft will tell you that the first-act break comes on page 30, the second on page 90 and the third on 120. There isn't one writer I've spoken with who follows that rigid paradigm. Warren Adler says it's "bullshit." James Toback calls it "utter formulaic madness." Darryl Ponicsan terms it "crippling," and Lowell Ganz says that he and partner Babaloo Mandel are known for their long first acts which break around page 40, allowing more time to establish the characters.

In fact, Toback doesn't even think about structure during the writing process. He believes in "letting a script take on its own reality and following it. Once I know who the characters are, what the world is and what the general idea of the story is I just let it go. I don't worry about where it's going. I don't worry if the characters are going to behave in a certain way. I just follow it."

As for Joe Eszterhas: "I just start writing. I don't know most of the time what's going to happen. I don't outline or plot it out before. I try to let it flow. I don't consciously adhere to a three-act structure, but intuitively I somehow feel the rhythms of where the story is going. I know the characters, but in terms of exactly what is going to happen from day to day, I don't know it, and that's one of the great joys of writing fiction."

"I let my characters find their way through the story," says Frank Pierson, "and I don't know most of the time how it's going to end at all. I find it out as I write it. There are some laws of story structure which tend to emerge in the process of writing, but what I start with is the character, and I don't worry about the structure at all. Nonetheless, there is a structure that tends to emerge."

Writer Mark Stein, on the other hand, strikes a balance between structure and craft, and instinct and improvisation. "I work in a three-act structure, and the first question I ask is what is this story going to be about? And however the idea begins for a story—whether it be a character, an arena, a situation, someone giving me an idea—the second question I ask is what is the ending? Because if I know this, then I find that the middle takes care of itself. I know where I'm going, and can start asking myself the right questions that yield the first-act break, second act crisis, and so on. Then at a certain point I let go, let some sort of spontaneity take over. Otherwise it's paint-by-number."

Ponicsan finds that "each project kind of dictates its own method of writing and construction. I find that I discover new techniques with every project I do. I work very strongly in the three-act structure, though I try not to make that transparent in the reading, that there are three clear divisions. I concentrate mostly on plot, and through the plot my characters will reveal themselves."

As for the argument that adhering to structure is beneath one's standing as an artist, "The biggest structuralist in the world was James Joyce," says writer Gary Ross. "He structured his stories with charts, logarithms and mathematical formulas. He was the most systematized writer that ever lived."

"Art is a matter of execution," says Nicholas Meyer (writer of TIME AFTER TIME, THE SEVEN-PERCENT SOLUTION, STAR TREK IV, STAR TREK VI). "It's a matter of what you do with it. I don't believe in art by accident. And if you want to break the so-called rules of structure, break them because you understand the consequences. Break them for an effect—to achieve what you want. Don't break them out of ignorance."

The following intensive examination of structure should provide some illumination.

This is essentially what the buyers look for:

THE FIRST ACT

—A story that ignites as quickly as possible and captures the reader's attention

—The introduction of an interesting, well-defined, dimensional protagonist we can genuinely care about and sympathize with

—A sense of urgency for the protagonist to make a personal change or rectify a situation

—A powerful inciting incident

—A clearly defined, compelling central conflict

—A formidable goal or quest for the protagonist

—The protagonist being forced to take action in pursuit of this goal from which s/he cannot be deterred

—Sufficient conflict and momentum en route to...

—A *climax/turning point* at the end of the first act which (*a*) creates a significant change in the life situation of a character (be it negative or positive); (*b*) brings the act to a pivotal/climactic moment; (*c*) launches the protagonist on a quest/journey; (*d*) paves the way for the confrontation to come in the second act

—*A reason to keep reading!*

A fine example of a beautifully written first act, containing all of these components, is found in THELMA & LOUISE, for which writer Callie Khouri garnered both the Oscar and Golden Globe Awards.

The elements of this story and how it is launched are well worth examining.

Catering to her controlling husband, who essentially treats her like a dimwitted slave, Thelma barely has a life of her own and has lacked the guts to break out.

A waitress in a coffee shop, Louise is tougher and more worldly but has yet to really do anything with her life. She also has man trouble in the form of a sexy but noncommittal boyfriend with a violent temper.

As every writer must, Khouri captures our attention in short order. Thelma and Louise (dual protagonists in the vein of Butch and Sundance) are engaging, sympathetic, clearly defined characters ripe for adventure. We're immediately drawn into their world and want to know more about them. We genuinely like them, and wonder how they're going to extricate themselves from their sad little lives.

Within the first five minutes of the film (which translates into about 5 script pages), Khouri instills in her characters a need (not merely a desire) for change. Hence there is a definite urgency to their situations; the story ignites and starts building early on, as it must. Anticipation is created. There is sufficient conflict. The writing isn't bogged down by dull, stagnant talk. We feel for and are intrigued by the characters.

As a protagonist must be an action-taking character, not merely reactive, Thelma and Louise then embark on a road trip to let their hair down and have some fun. We know they're in for more than they bargained for. As in any good story, what the character anticipates will happen turns out to be just the opposite. In other words, *more conflict is injected.*

Deftly setting up what will be the pivotal turning point of the first act, Khouri soon plunges her characters head-on into *jeopardy*, a critical ingredient in any good story, comedy or drama. At a roadside bar, Thelma and Louise's world is turned upside down. Thelma is brutally raped in the parking lot and Louise kills the rapist. These two events (the rape and murder) comprise the INCITING INCIDENT.

Typically occurring within the first 5 to 30 pages, the inciting incident must be strong enough to accomplish several things: throw the protagonist's life radically (not mildly) off course; give way to the central conflict; heighten the stakes; send the protagonist in pursuit of a goal from which he or she cannot be deterred; give way to a substantive and compelling *Central Question* that will run through the story until it's answered in the resolution. The writer must raise as much suspense as to the outcome of this question as possible. If it's too soft and weak, the reader will quickly lose interest in the plight of the protagonist.

In THELMA & LOUISE, the stakes of the central question are extremely high as we wonder: Will they outrun the police or get caught? Suspense is continually heightened as the women plunge ever deeper into danger until ultimately their very lives hang in the balance.

Referring back to the inciting incident, notice what it accomplishes in the first act. After Thelma is raped and Louise kills the guy, their lives are thrown completely off-balance; anything less than that and the inciting incident is too soft. The central conflict then becomes the women vs. the law, and they are accordingly launched on a quest, in pursuit of a goal from which they cannot be deterred: outrun the cops or face terrible consequences. If the goal is too slight—if it isn't something which the protagonist absolutely must pursue—there isn't enough urgency to the situation and the story will be weakened as a result.

The point at which this goal is set into motion becomes the FIRST ACT CLIMAX: Thelma and Louise flee the rape/murder scene and hightail it down the road.

Now here's the clincher. A pair of seemingly ordinary women simply looking to have fun are suddenly fugitives on the run. A dramatic change (negative or positive) has occurred in the life situation of the characters, the first act dynamically leading into the second.

THE SECOND ACT

The second act is the longest act in a three-act story (typically twice as long as the first and third). And it is here that most scripts fall apart. The story begins to sag and is saddled with some or all of the following: uninvolving, episodic scenes, lightweight turning points, page-long speeches that do nothing but take up space, unbelievable coincidences, confusing or inexplicable events, little or no drive and momentum.

The reader steadily loses interest in the script, and unless the concept and characters are strong enough to compensate for glaring structural weaknesses, the script is sent packing.

A good second act should:

—Build in a sturdy progression

—Have a strong upward momentum and a sense of increasing conflict, urgency, tension

—Create compelling obstacles/complications which continually threaten and thwart the protagonist

—Force the protagonist to take greater and greater actions in pursuit of his/her goal

—Show evidence that the protagonist is gradually changing, growing, evolving

—Not be propelled by talk

—Not be repetitive, obvious, predictable

—Sustain the reader's interest and emotional involvement

—Hook and hold the reader en route to a riveting climax greater in intensity than the first act climax but not as great as the third

—IT MUST MOVE!

In THELMA & LOUISE, Khouri keeps the second act moving by gradually heightening the conflict, increasing the tension, raising the stakes, and plunging her characters into greater degrees of risk and jeopardy.

Louise, broke, is forced to ask her boyfriend Jimmy for money. The women plan to cross the border into Mexico, a long and dangerous drive, while a police investigation gets underway. Thelma sleeps with J.D., a young hitchhiker/crook who leaves the women high and dry. Thelma robs a convenience store: now they have money again but are wanted for both murder and armed robbery. A tape of the robbery is viewed by police with Thelma's husband Darryl, whose home becomes the center of police activity and is equipped with phone-tapping equipment. The police interrogate Jimmy to learn the women's whereabouts. J.D. is arrested and brought in for questioning, tipping the police off that Thelma and Louise were last in Oklahoma City and are headed for Mexico. Thelma suspects that Louise was raped in Texas some time ago (given her violent explosion of rage toward Thelma's rapist), but Louise orders the subject dropped. They're repeatedly harassed by a horny trucker in a semi-tanker, and then stopped by a highway patrolman who could easily throw them in jail. Training a gun on him, Thelma orders the patrolman into the trunk of his car as Louise shoots his radio and drills the trunk full of air holes. Louise phones the police at Darryl's house, learning from detective Hal that she and Thelma will be charged with murder unless they turn themselves in. When Louise refuses, the stakes are upped even higher by the police, who essentially give Thelma and Louise a choice of coming out of this dead or alive. Then the stakes are upped even higher when the police trace Louise's phone call.

This becomes the SECOND ACT CLIMAX, the point at which the protagonist must make a pivotal decision that will affect his or her life and the outcome of the story.

The crisis must carry tremendous weight for both the protagonist and the audience on an emotional level. If the crisis is too slight, as in many substandard scripts—if what the protagonist is grappling with doesn't carry enough weight—emotional involvement is severely curtailed and the script is diluted.

But that isn't the case with Thelma and Louise, whose crisis decision is nothing less than freedom vs. entrapment: Do they keep on running or turn themselves in? More importantly, do they come out of this dead or alive? Because turning themselves in would go against the very nature of their characters by this point, providing evidence of how far they have evolved from the beginning, they do what they must and decide to go on.

In doing so, conflict is heightened; tension and suspense are raised; our emotional investment in the characters is stronger; the levels of risk and jeopardy are increased and hard-driving momentum propels the story into the third act—which reaches the highest climactic levels of all.

Note, too, that Khouri creates a carefully orchestrated *rhythm* in the second act. The action rises and falls: building to a certain point of tension, falling just enough to create a temporary lull in the action, but not so far that momentum is lost altogether. Then it rises again, a bit higher than before, and falls—the pattern repeated throughout while still maintaining sufficient drive and excitement.

This is illustrated in THELMA & LOUISE when the hard-driving build is interspersed with picturesque shots of the landscape, the women driving in silence, contemplating their fate, talking and singing, shots of the police sitting in silence waiting for the phone to ring. Such carefully orchestrated lulls in the action add texture to the story, allow time for reflection, more emotion to seep in, and create through a series of highs and lows a smooth structural rhythm. If executed properly and with finesse, and the pace is not slowed down so long that the story loses energy, these periodic shifts in tempo will add dimension to and enhance your script overall.

THE THIRD ACT

The act in which the dramatic tension is brought to its highest point and the central conflict resolved, the third act must:

—Not be short-changed, rushed, or ended too abruptly

—Be infused with sufficient conflict, tension, and urgency

—Build to a climactic point before the resolution

—Pit the protagonist against the antagonist/forces of opposition

—Provide evidence of a character arc: a definite change in the protagonist from what s/he was at the outset

—Not leave a mass of loose ends dangling

—Not be blatantly obvious or predictably pat

—Not be so ambiguous that the resolution is too vague or obscure

—Provide a payoff for the audience: an ending that gives them what they want, but not in the exact way they expect

The third act of THELMA & LOUISE begins as the outcome of the crisis decision: they're still determined to keep on running and make it to Mexico. Logically stemming from this decision, the CLIMAX is played out as Thelma and Louise desperately, futilely try to outrun the police.

But as in any well-structured story, even bigger obstacles are thrown in their way to deter them from their goal. Thelma and Louise are pushed further and further into a corner from which there is no escape.

Nearing the end of their rope, they again encounter the horny trucker, who goes too far this time as Thelma and Louise blow up his semi-tanker. Louise then admits that Thelma was right: Louise was raped in Texas some time ago, hence her violent actions toward Thelma's attacker at the outset. They then make one last run for it, but to no avail as an army of cops is ready to arrest them or gun them down. It is here that the THIRD ACT CLIMAX is reached. Thelma and Louise are now faced with the toughest decision of their lives: to turn themselves in or keep going.

But because the third act climax must be greater in intensity than the second, to keep on going this time means driving their car over the Grand Canyon to a fiery death. The beauty and irony of this, however, is that death actually holds more freedom than life for Thelma and Louise, who haven't come this far and risked so much to let men or the law dictate whether they will live or die, be free or sentenced to life in prison. So they choose the only alternative that is reasonable and right for them: death. A tearful hug, the clutching of hands, Louise gunning the engine—and off they go over the cliff, the shot freezing them in mid-air. This is, of course, the RESOLUTION.

In examining this three-act structure, note the connection between crisis, climax and resolution. A pivotal decision is made (typically at the end of the second act) which monumentally affects the life of the protagonist and the outcome of the story. This gives way to the climax (climactic action), which ultimately yields the resolution.

Also note that the second act climax, whether it be negative or positive, will *contrast* with the resolution. So if the second act ends up (positively for the protagonist), the story will end down (negatively). If the second act ends down, the story will have a happy ending, which is indicative of virtually every film in the Hollywood mainstream.

Applying this principle to THELMA & LOUSE, the second act ends with them vowing to keep going—and the ending of the film, brimming with irony, has both a positive and negative charge: positive in the sense that they'll retain control of their destinies and die together, yet negative because they have to lose their lives to do it. Not all stories will have or require this type of double-edged ending; but in this case it reinforces the irony, enhances the meaning, and serves the story beautifully. Watching Thelma and Louise drive off that cliff, you're crying and cheering at the same time.

112

In THELMA & LOUISE, the arc of both protagonists is very definite, clear and strong. They're initially presented as women who play by the rules and lead controlled, restricted lives. They haven't had the guts to risk and really orchestrate their own destinies, particularly Thelma, and have generally rolled with the punches instead of creating their own opportunities.

But Louise's killing of the rapist begins to change all that, and as she and Thelma arc through the story, they ultimately emerge as tough, ball-busting, fiercely independent women who not only don't take s—t from anyone, they'd rather die in the name of freedom than allow the law to dictate their lives.

Again, we'll discuss more of this in the following chapter, but suffice to say that the protagonist must arc through the story in some fashion (some more than others), and how he has evolved must be evident by the end of the third act lest it be cited by the reader as a structural flaw.

Also note that the central question is answered in the OBLIGATORY SCENE—the scene that must take place before the story can be resolved. The protagonist must engage in a final confrontation with the antagonist in which one emerges victorious and the other defeated. You couldn't, in other words, write the obligatory scene for THELMA & LOUISE in which they are not facing an army of policemen.

Also be aware that if the protagonist emerges triumphant in the end too quickly and easily, merely struggling here and there throughout the story amidst minimal conflict, the obligatory scene will be anticlimactic and we'll feel cheated by the protagonist's final victory. The result: no payoff. And if the protagonist is defeated in the end but was never given much of a chance— the conflict so overwhelming that she is a loser from the start— again we'll feel cheated and there is no payoff.

To achieve the right balance is critical, and the above weaknesses can *only* be avoided if a story arrives at its resolution via the proper structure. In other words, the progression of scenes throughout a script must be structured to gradually set up and pave the way for the final payoff. So if you traced your story backwards, you should find that the resolution is the logical, sat-isfying, deftly crafted culmination of everything preceding it and that every scene is working in service of the final payoff. No scenes occur accidentally in a well-structured story. If any scene is just there for the heck of it, it doesn't belong in your script.

Now that you have an idea of what the critical elements are in a three-act structure, let's look at the most common reasons why screenplays fail structurally and are rejected.

STRUCTURE WITHIN A SCENE

Just as there must be a structure to the overall construction of a story, so must there be within a scene. Yet this is a fact which eludes many writers whose screenplays are littered with pointless filler scenes that don't propel the story. Often there is no move-ment or conflict within these scenes, and because they serve absolutely no purpose to either the story or characters, they could just as well be cut.

Says screenwriter Leslie Dixon, "Either a script reads enter-tainingly and there's a purpose to each scene, or there isn't. And if there isn't a purpose to a scene, it shouldn't be there. If some-thing hasn't changed at the end of the scene from where it began, you're probably not doing your job."

You must continually question whether a scene you're writing is actually adding to the story or just cluttering it. What reason is there for this scene to take place? What purpose it is serving in moving the characters through the story? Is it helping to advance the plot? Moreover, what is actually taking place *within* the scene? And if the answer to this question isn't something significant to the story and characters, either enhance it or pull it out of your script.

CONFLICT

The essence of good storytelling is conflict. Without it a script stops moving. Period. Once the reader becomes bored and starts skimming, the script is as good as gone.

Whether it takes the form of *personal conflict* (man vs. man), *inner conflict* (man vs. himself), *extrapersonal conflict* (man vs.

society, his physical environment, the forces of nature, etc.) or exists on all three levels, conflict is what drives a script and it must be there in abundance.

In many failed scripts, however, there is a dearth of conflict from page to page as stagnant, vacuous dialogue overrides plot. There is no momentum, the writer missing obvious opportunities to turn up the heat and increase the stakes. The reader waits for the story to ignite, but as one lifeless page follows another, quickly loses interest.

Says Bennett Schneir, a story analyst for Imagine Films Entertainment, "When I read a script, I immediately question where the conflict is. Where's the conflict in this act, this scene, this story? But some scripts will go 45-50 pages and there's no conflict. Nothing is going on. Everyone agrees with each other. One character will say, 'Let's do this,' and then everyone says 'OK!'

"Or there are stories where the conflict is too soft. I read a script about the son of a wealthy man who wants him to join the family diamond business, but the son wants to become an architect. That's the entire story...and who cares?"

In other scripts, the conflict kicks in too late.

Says writer Tom Schulman, "Something really important and devastating has to have happened to the protagonist by the end of the first curtain. If it hasn't happened by 20, 30, 40 minutes into the film—and 40 is late—then something isn't right. After the first act, things must continue to happen. If it's been 2 1/2 pages and the conflict is dying down, a sort of internal timer should say to you that it's time for something to happen. You're always inventing new conflicts to test the main character."

Not that conflicts are injected according to page numbers ("I have never in my life said it's page 42, time to have an explosion," says Leslie Dixon), but a writer should be so tuned in to the momentum of a script that he realizes when things are slowing down and its time to jack up the conflict.

But the problem with many rejected scripts is not only a lack of conflict but *repeated* conflicts, the writer running out of ideas and rehashing the same conflicts over and over again.

A man is on the run from the mob in an action/comedy, for instance, and the next 75 pages have him doing the same thing: hiding out in a series of motels, hitchhiking, engaging in shootouts with the mobsters and taking off again—but nothing *new* happens.

You must have a constant flow of *new information*—new conflicts, new twists and turns—new SOMETHING! You want your script to move boom, boom, boom—always turning, turning, turning. First the man hides out in a motel and hitchhikes to the next town, but then something happens! Suddenly he's on the front page of every newspaper as a "Wanted" man, the mobsters wielding their influence to frame him for a murder he didn't commit. This, of course, creates a whole slew of new problems for him to contend with, because now he has to get a disguise—which leads to another problem because at the airport someone mistakes him for a visiting French dignitary and says he's late for a meeting at the embassy...just as the mobsters recognize him and give chase.

Each conflict leads to another without repetition, the character forced to take new actions and overcome new and more difficult challenges. A steady infusion of *new conflicts* that turn the script—that is key.

Says Imagine Films story analyst Seth Miller, "I tend to pass on scripts which by page 20 or 30, don't seem to be getting anywhere. The stories go off on tangents or stay in the same place; nothing seems to be changing. Good stories always keep turning."

Many writers fail to employ *reversals* to heighten the conflict. A reversal is a 180-degree change in the life situation of a character: rich to poor, married to unmarried, hopeful to hopeless. When well placed, reversals sink the protagonist deeper into trouble, building the tension and the audience's involvement.

This progression—the difference between what the character anticipates will happen and what actually happens, the difference between what the character assumes will be necessary to accomplish his goal and the actual struggle it takes to achieve it—that is the so-called "stuff" of drama. It is where the conflict lies in a script, and the process by which the stakes are raised and momentum is increased.

You also want to avoid forced, mechanical conflict which isn't organic to the story or characters.

Says executive Andrea Asimow, "I read so many scripts in which the conflict is so artificial. The writer needs to have a conflict so they think of something that seems kind of pasted on, and that turns me off immediately. But when a conflict seems to spring from who the characters are and their condition in the world the writer has created, I'm right there."

Some writers just throw the conflicts in as if they're somehow separate from the characters, not realizing that the two are intertwined. The danger of that, explains writer Gary Ross, is that "you are externally manipulating events and forcing your characters to do something that they wouldn't intrinsically or inherently do. You're intruding upon the story to manipulate it for your own purposes, and that pisses off an audience because they feel manipulated. Many writers write from a mechanical place. They say now we need a crisis, well...what that can be? But they're artificially manipulating events to lead up to that point."

So while a script will be faulted for having a shortage of conflict, it will also get nailed if the conflict seems phony. Even though your script may be packed with conflicts, the only way to avoid such phoniness is to have the conflict originate from the actions of the characters.

It might help to think in terms of *causality*. Just as there must be causality in a script from scene to scene, each causing the next in a logical, cohesive progression (thereby alleviating the problem of coincidence), so must there be a *causal* link between the conflicts or progressive complications, and the actions of your characters. The characters cause the conflicts to occur, not the needs of the writer to keep his protagonist in hot water.

SETUPS & PAYOFFS

Just as the overall progression of scenes in a well-structured screenplay gradually sets up and works in service of the final

117

payoff, so must the writer pay attention to individual setups and payoffs within a script.

In FATAL ATTRACTION, for instance, the scene in which the little girl's pet rabbit is found boiling on the stove is deftly set up beforehand. Early in the film it is established how badly the girl wants a rabbit. Then her parents discuss the issue: Should they buy her a rabbit? And once they buy the rabbit, a lot of care is taken in the film as to how they'll present it to their daughter. If you recall, the father sneaks it home in a cage to surprise the girl, thus driving home the fact that this rabbit is *very, very special* to her.

Why go to all this trouble to set up a bond between the daughter and the rabbit? Because it makes the "dead rabbit" scene that much more powerful. The audience feels terribly for the little girl, knowing how much she wanted and loved the rabbit, and it makes the actions of the villain Alex that much more sinister. Moreover, the dead rabbit is used symbolically to set up Alex's shocking confession to Dan that she is pregnant with his child.

But without the setup beforehand, the dead rabbit wouldn't have had nearly as much meaning, emotion and shock value— which is precisely where many substandard writers go wrong. They don't take the time to set up pivotal scenes, thereby diminishing their effect.

Another example is found in the film SAY ANYTHING, by writer-director Cameron Crowe. There's a scene in which Diane (Ione Skye) is being pressured by her father (John Mahoney) to break up with Lloyd (John Cusack), and the father suggests giving him a pen as a token parting gift. Diane is stunned, saying, in effect, that in a million years she would never think of giving Lloyd something as trivial and meaningless as a pen.

Now this scene isn't in the script because the writer felt like throwing in some extra conflict. Rather, it is a scene that *sets up* the *payoff* in which Diane does, in fact, give Lloyd a pen as she breaks up with him. Now it is Lloyd who's stunned. Here he has fallen head over heels in love with the girl of his dreams, only to be dumped and, on top of that, be given something as trivial and meaningless as a pen.

Says producer Lauren Shuler-Donner, "A problem I often find in scripts is that nothing is set up or paid off properly. Either the situations are set up but never paid off, or paid off but never set up...

"It's like show the banana, show the banana—and then somebody slips on the banana. That's the payoff."

So a good writer paves the way for the occurence of key scenes and turning points so they'll pay off with sufficient force and meaning.

TALKINESS & VISUALITY

A script will also get nailed for being too talky, the writer propelling the plot through stagnant, lifeless dialogue instead of *conflict, action*, and *behavior*. The characters talk more than they act, rambling on about their lives, each other, what they've done, what they're going to do, what they want—and who cares! The writer is committing the sin of telling more than showing, and the effect is dismal.

Your job is to put images in the reader's head, not merely convey your story with words. If anything, cut down on talk and be as visually evocative as you can. You must show events as they occur, not have them robotically spewed from the characters' mouths. Readers don't want to hear your story being told, we want to see it! *Make things happen visually!*

If you're writing a thriller, let's actually see the murder as it happens, not merely hear someone tell the police about it after the fact. By then it's too late, the excitement is over. But many bad writers will do just that; they'll include a murder and play it off-screen, revealing the details through mounds of talk. The result: talk overrides plot, the visuality is nil, the suspense is gone, and that's how scripts get passed on.

Granted, there are times when a speech or monologue is necessary. There's a monologue in THE FISHER KING (by Richard LaGravenese) in which Parry (Robin Williams) conveys to Jack (Jeff Bridges) the history of the Fisher King and the Holy Grail. But the difference between this monologue and those found in bad scripts is that it does not impede the flow of the story. The

119

words don't lie there on the page like a dead fish, and Parry isn't used merely as a mouthpiece to move the plot along. Rather, the monologue reflects his passion and excitement and is perfectly suited to his character. That isn't talky; that's just good writing.

But when a script comes in with a ton of excess verbiage and just seems bloated with words—when pages and pages go by with absolutely nothing happening but one conversation after another—it becomes clear that we're dealing with an amateur who doesn't know structure.

The good writer reveals information not through words, but through *conflict*. Perhaps a daughter is shocked to discover from a relative that she was adopted. She angrily confronts her mother, who emphatically denies the truth. She then discovers her mother burning the adoption papers in the middle of the night, leading to an explosive conflict between mother and daughter as the truth comes out through their screaming and tears.

Another problem in many scripts is the dreaded "instant relationship" between two strangers, who not only come together quite unbelievably, but let loose with verbal autobiographies that stop the story cold. Even worse is when the strangers have just had mad, passionate sex and then lie there, like two formless blobs, shedding light on their turbulent pasts. "So tell me about yourself, Bobbie," says the man, drenched in sweat. "It's Betty," says the woman, blowing smoke rings into the air. "Well, I was born in a small town in Nebraska. My father drank too much and left us high and dry, my mother working as a circus clown and a seamstress to support us ten kids."

Well, that's too bad, Betty, but does anyone in their right mind care what you're saying? No, because amidst all your blabbing the story has stopped. Such scenes are dreadful on the page because you don't care a whit about the characters and the talk is devoid of meaning.

Again, had the writer injected conflict into the scene, perhaps having the man threaten to hurl Betty into a pond of piranhas unless she reveals a key piece of information from her past, then what was stagnant talk would suddenly have urgency and meaning.

There is vacuous talk that deadens a script and *electric, explosive* talk that breathes life into every page. If your characters are talking their heads off like robotic encyclopedias...PASS.

PREDICTABILITY

Most stories operate with a certain degree of inevitability which the reader will tolerate. For example, it's inevitable in PRETTY WOMAN and WHEN HARRY MET SALLY...that the lovers will reconcile in the end. In fact, we'd be disappointed if they didn't. It's inevitable that the hero in DIE HARD will defeat the terrorists, and inevitable in TERMS OF ENDEARMENT that the daughter will die of cancer.

But there is a big difference between anticipating the outcome of a well-structured story, and predictability due to the writer's lack of invention.

"Structure is necessary but not sufficient," says Steel Pictures' Jordi Ros, "because a lot of writers confuse structure with formula. And formula means that the reader knows exactly where the story is going by page 10, and by then I usually stop reading. I know where it's going and I don't want to go there. I've been there before."

Adds Martha Browning, a story analyst for Morgan Creek (ROBIN HOOD: PRINCE OF THIEVES), "I've read so many scripts that it's more difficult for a writer to take me where I don't expect to go—and that is what I look for. I want to be surprised, and it's really hard to surprise someone like me by now."

Amblin's Jason Hoffs wants a script "that makes me go 'Wow.' Something that makes me smile, makes me cry...that indicates that I'm not reading one dead, leaden, predictable page after the next. I want something interesting, stimulating, different, cool, weird..."

But so often, says Hoffs, "I read it and I'm not engaged. I'm not brought into that world. The elements are predictable. We've seen these characters before, their problems and motivations."

So if your script is headed toward a conclusion we inevitably know is coming, which is fine, you absolutely cannot afford to go with the first thing that pops into your head, which is probably the most predictable. Always try to spin a script in unexpected directions. Take great pains to avoid one of those predictably pat endings with a pretty little bow around it.

Says writer Jeb Stuart (DIE HARD, ANOTHER 48 HRS., among others), "Turn scenes in the opposite direction they would predictably go in and reverse the reader's expectations. But to lay it out so coldly, like a slab, that's when the bells and whistles should start going off in your head and you're thinking, 'Isn't there something else I can do to make it less obvious?'"

SUBPLOTS

A subplot is a story line which is secondary or subordinate to the main plot.

Some scripts have a single subplot, such as the Chevy Chase/Goldie Hawn comedy FOUL PLAY in which there is a murder main plot and a romantic subplot.

Other scripts branch off into several subplots, such as DIRTY DANCING. The main plot is the coming-of-age of Baby (Jennifer Grey) and her romance with Johnny (Patrick Swayze) at a summer resort. The subplots include Baby's relationship with her father, competition with her sister, the sister's short-lived romance with a sleazy waiter, and the botched abortion of a dancer who's impregnated by the waiter.

But whether a script contains one subplot or ten isn't the issue. The point is that each and every subplot in a script must intersect at some point with both the protagonist *and* the main plot—creating new levels of conflict, adding dimension and texture to the story, and complicating the plight of the protagonist.

In many poorly structured scripts, the subplots tend to dangle in the middle of nowhere and exist parallel to the main plot, never meshing with it or the protagonist. This creates a convoluted, tangential feel, the script veering into various directions which aren't in sync with the main plot.

Sometimes the subplot reads more like another main plot, as if the writer were juggling two different films within the same script. Both involve the protagonist, yet the script is pulled in two different directions. Other subplots are set up but not followed through, the writer letting them drop and hoping no one will notice. Believe me, they'll notice.

While subplots can add dimension and complexity to a script, they should clearly and effectively tie in with the main plot and protagonist. They must have a definite purpose and, very importantly, must be resolved instead of disintegrating in the middle for no apparent reason. You don't want the reader to go searching through the script for the loose ends you've left hanging, only to come up empty-handed.

COINCIDENCE & CONVENIENCE

Another reason scripts are passed on is an abundance of *coincidence*. This can rob a script of credibility. While the argument can certainly be made that because there is coincidence in life it is therefore acceptable in a script, that is only true to a certain extent. For I've read many a script in which the plot turns are painfully contrived because they're too coincidental to be believed.

For instance, a character who's about to declare bankruptcy and lose his house *just happens* to find a bag of money under the seat in a taxi. A character who's lost in the middle of nowhere *just happens* to find an unattended car...with keys inside! Such coincidences are always unbelievable and come off as far too *convenient*.

How *utterly convenient* that Millie, who only that morning was dreaming of romance, just happens to get into a car accident with a man who thinks she's the most wonderful woman in the world. *How convenient* that police detective Billingsley, for weeks on the tail of a crook who's busted out of the slammer, just happens to meet someone in a bar who roomed with the crook in college and remembers he had a cabin in the woods.

Keep these farfetched, heavy-handed coincidences out of your scripts. Sure, in a zany comedy a few coincidences are perfectly fine. Others may simply reflect life. In MANHATTAN, it's a coincidence that Isaac (Woody Allen) and Mary (Diane Keaton) bump into each other at a party one night, the incident then paving the way for romance. But that sort of thing just happens in life and is not the kind of coincidence that strains credibility.

What I'm taking about are those huge, laughably implausible coincidences which just aren't real. They don't come about naturally, but rather are used by bad writers to oh-so-conveniently move the plot along. They read phony and should be avoided at all costs.

TELLING MORE OFF-SCREEN THAN ON

A huge mistake made by some amateur writers is conveying important information in the off-camera directions never made available to the audience. Describing in great detail, say, a set of family photographs, but failing to incorporate that information into the body of the script, is a major error. The person reading the script knows that a character is a freelance photographer named Bill who still has nightmares about Vietnam, but the *audience* doesn't learn any of this because the writer has only conveyed it *off screen*.

I've also read scripts that don't convey to the audience how the story is resolved. One in particular was a murder/whodunnit in which the entire motive for the killing was contained in the off-camera directions. The audience would walk out of the theater, never knowing the reasoning behind the killer's actions and why the murder took place.

Says Martha Browning, "It's almost as if these people haven't read their scripts before they send them out. I've read scripts that would need to give the audience a chart to take into the theater with them. I've said in my coverage that if the audience didn't have a blueprint and a family tree they'd never know what was going on."

So do yourself a favor: *Be professional. Do not conceal in the off-camera directions important information the audience needs to know.* This can be a surefire cause of rejection.

CONFUSING THE READER

Perhaps worse than leaving the audience in the dark is omitting information the reader needs to know to fully comprehend your script. Don't make the person go on a scavenger hunt to figure out who the characters are, what they do, why they do it, how they know each other, what they're talking about, where the story is going, where it takes place. That'll get you a PASS as fast as anything I know.

Although you want to write as *leanly* as possible and not overload your script with too much detail and explanation, you must make sure that whomever is reading your script knows *exactly* what it contains and what it's about.

Structure it so that everything is clear, well-defined, and precise. Be meticulous in your writing, always questioning whether something is vague and won't be understood. Give your script *direction*. Give it a logical, causal, cohesive flow. Avoid at all costs baffling the reader.

A RECAP

—A poorly structured script, even if it contains some viable elements, is likely to be rejected

—Adhere to proper script construction without becoming mechanical or formulaic

—Buyers look for a three-act structure: beginning, middle, and end

—The first act must hook the reader early on, giving way to a compelling central conflict and building to a climax

—The second act must contain sufficient conflict and drive, placing the protagonist more at risk as it builds to an even higher climax

—The third act builds to the highest climactic level of all and resolves the story—satisfying the audience, but not exactly in the way they expect

—Scripts get passed on due to artificial or too little conflict; an abundance of stagnant talk; blatant predictability; lack of invention; heavy-handed coincidence; unrelated subplots; lack of direction; vague, illogical plotting that confuses the reader and disregards the audience.

6

Character

Virtually all of the screenwriters I've interviewed for this book feel that *character* is the true essence of writing.

Says James Toback, "I'm always thinking of character first. Who is this movie about? I think character is everything if one is talking about a movie being seen more than once; and if I really thought that a movie I was conceiving wasn't going to be worth seeing more than once, nothing in the world could get me to bother going ahead with it. Once you've said that plot is the most important thing, what you're really saying is that there's no point in seeing the movie again. Why see it again if you already know what's going to happen? Seeing it again is only viable if what you're getting from it goes beyond what's on the surface, and plot is just surface, just events."

"It begins for us with character," says writer Lowell Ganz (partner with Babaloo Mandel). "Before we start to write a movie, we know who the characters are and must be able to hear them. In building the plot we talk to each other in the voices of the characters. We can always find a plot or concept for a movie, but the key for us is always character."

"Getting the protagonist from point A to point Z, that's what a story's about," says writer Tom Schulman. "You're sort of peeling off the layers of what the character is feeling, what they want, what motivates them, what makes them tick, what they're going through. What you're doing, in essence, is involving the audience in the drama of other people's lives. And we all love that."

These sentiments are echoed by the executives.

"If someone tells me they have a great script," says Paramount's Margaret French, "for me it's not about the plot or necessarily the genre; it's more about what happens to the characters—their growth and what they need to overcome. So if someone pitches me an idea, I don't need to hear every single beat of the story; I need to know how the characters change, what their progression is, what they learn through the course of the story. That's what is most important to me."

Says David Bruskin, director of development for producer Laura Ziskin (HERO, PRETTY WOMAN, WHAT ABOUT BOB?, THE DOCTOR, NO WAY OUT), "For me, the heart of a screenplay is the characters. Do I emotionally respond to them? Because if the answer is yes, then we have a lot to go on. And if it's no, then it's almost done right there."

Adds Amblin's Jason Hoffs, "No matter what the genre—no matter how broad—who the characters are, what they go through and how they change is, to me, what brings a screenplay to life. No matter what kind of movie you're making, I think it's best to think first in terms of the character. In LETHAL WEAPON, it's not just bang-bang, shoot 'em up, but it's about a guy who really wants to kill himself at the beginning because he's lost everything and finds a reason to live at the end."

Says Hoffs of the planned film version of MR. MAGOO (a co-production between Amblin and Warner Bros.), "He's a very idealistic, quixotic character who doesn't always happen to see the world as it really is but triumphs at the end because of his idealism. We want to make that movie, and it just happens to be about Mr. Magoo."

As for story analyst Martha Browning: "I tend to be more interested in character than the story, or sometimes even the premise. A script may come in with a lot of flaws, but if there is a character that has an emotional resonance and I feel something, I'll be much more enthusiastic in my coverage and say, 'Look out for this writer's next script. Let her send another one...'"

There is no denying the critical importance of character, yet so many writers fail to bring their characters to life on the page. The writer doesn't make us care. And the minute you stop caring about the characters, you're no longer involved in the story. Character is plot and plot is character. They are linked.

Says Susan Morgan Williams, "You have to weave a character into the story to keep the audience caring and watching, wanting to see the resolution of that character—not the story. Not that the story isn't a crucial element, but it has to work in tandem with the character."

THE PLOT/CHARACTER CONNECTION

As the plot unfolds, it places a specific set of pressures and conflicts upon the character, who then takes a specific course of action in reaction to those conflicts. But if the plot were any different, so would the actions of the character change accordingly. If the plot to SOPHIE'S CHOICE were any different, then Sophie would never have had to make the excruciating choice of which of her two children would accompany her into Auschwitz and which would be sent to the Birkenau crematorium.

At the same time, the plot evolves from the actions and inherent nature of the characters. If the character of Jack in THE FISHER KING chose not to get the Holy Grail for Parry, that single decision would have forced the writer to come up with an entirely different third act.

By linking your characters to the plot, you're in a better position to recognize narrative actions which don't seem true to the characters. You'll be more apt to question why your characters do what they do.

Says Gregory Avellone of Tig Productions (Kevin Costner's company), "To get themselves in and out of scenes, writers will do something that just doesn't come from reality; it's just a way to get them on to the next scene. They'll throw something in that goes against the grain of their characters, and that aggravates me because it's not believable. It's not a logical transition."

Adds executive-turned-screenwriter Matt Tabak, "When I read in a cop script that someone teams up with so and so, I'm already pounding my head against the wall because it's already such an overly familiar device. But when it's such a random pairing of characters, like 'schoolteacher from small town in Connecticut teams up with jewel thief from Honduras,' I think that is so contrived to begin with that it's just not real."

The industry wants characters who are real and believable, and plotting that works in tandem with the characters. But let's be even more specific: What does Hollywood *really* want in your characters?

CHARACTER POSITIVES

Producer Lauren Shuler-Donner wants "characters that are unique and very strong, characters you can care about and root for, characters who are fleshed out and original—not cliched like a cop eating a doughnut. I look for characters whose motivations are clear yet complex, characters with conflict and many layers."

"Tell me something about a character that surprises me," says agent Geoff Sanford. "If you turned a camera on an unsuspecting person, something would be interesting and fascinating—their idiosyncratic bits of uniqueness that come through. That's what I want in a character. When you read a great piece of writing, there is something about the character that has even more than verisimilitude. There is something different about the character that is not a homogenized, Hollywood view. Then I become interested."

Susan Morgan Williams wants characters "textured enough that we would want to go on their journey with them, that we would care enough about the struggle or voyage they're going on." She wants a protagonist to "learn something through the course of the story. He doesn't necessarily have to make the world a better place, but if he has changed his life and somehow educated us about human nature or the psyche of man, that's essentially what I look for."

As for Andrea Asimow, "Every time I read a script, I look for the characters who feel real enough that I might meet them. Are there little connections between me and this character?"

Gregory Avellone wants to see characters "overcome their internal flaw and the outside odds that have been thrust upon them." He also wants "everything the protagonist does to come out of something real—something the audience can relate to. That's really how you can bring an audience to the edge of their seat because you're not trying to con them. Audiences are so smart today that they can tell, even in a trailer, if they're being conned."

Of course the demands of a protagonist are somewhat different depending on the genre. While the lead character must always be deftly-drawn and dimensional, you couldn't realistically say that Wayne in WAYNE'S WORLD educated us about human nature or the psyche of man.

But the point is that great characters, no matter what the story or genre, will score big points in a screenplay's favor. When someone is on the fence about a project, it could very well be the characters that keep it from being rejected out of hand.

CASTABILITY

What the industry also wants are castable characters—or, more specifically, *star roles*. Hollywood is star-driven, and you increase your chances of selling a script and getting it made if it offers enticing roles that stars want to play.

"That's the way you generate lightning in this business," says writer Larry Ferguson. "Stars can get movies made. If you write a script that nobody wants to read, but Robert DeNiro picks it up and says I want to play this part...guess what? You've got a deal. There aren't many directors in this world who can make that happen, but a lot of stars who can."

"Is the script castable?" queries Universal's Leonard Kornberg. "If the protagonist is the average Joe Shmoe who doesn't really change a lot, nor does he have any particularly emotional scenes or anything unusual to do, that's not castable. So is there something in this character that might draw a star? What is it about this character that is going to attract a star who's being offered everything that's out there? What might a star find in this role? That's where the studios are coming from. That's the reality."

So take great pains to imbue your leading roles with the uniqueness, power, dynamic qualities, sensibilities and complexities that make them star roles.

Says Gareth Wigan, executive production consultant for Columbia Pictures, "I think what you're looking for are characters that will attract the best actors, not just because names sell movies, but because good acting is one of the important things that sells movies. There are times when you'll read a 'difficult' project in which you realize there's no point in making this film unless you can find a wonderful actor to play that role. And in many cases that means it has to be played by a star, because it's not an accident that stars are often our best actors."

Adds Lauren Shuler-Donner, "You really have to look forward while you're developing a screenplay. You want compelling characters that hold your interest, but you ultimately have to think of how to cast the movie. And if you have created a full-blown, complex, interesting, conflicted character, be it comedic or dramatic, then chances are a fine actor will be drawn to it."

CHARACTER NEGATIVES

Many poorly conceived characters exist on one level only, consisting of nothing more than their surface characteristics. Such characters are virtually impossible to feel for, unlike real people who have various sides and layers to their emotional, psychological and intellectual selves. They don't have facets or layers to uncover because the writer has approached them externally and mechanically, not internally and dimensionally.

131

Some writers don't even give their characters names, labeling them instead according to type: MOTHER, FATHER, THUG #1, CROOK #6, etc. True, certain minor characters—a bank teller for instance—needn't be identified by name if he's simply fulfilling a societal function and nothing more. That's fine. But characters who become entwined in the plot, even for a short time, need real identities, not merely labels.

Says writer Leslie Dixon, "A common flaw in many, many scripts is that they don't have enough fleshed-out characters. I'm a big believer in subplots and minor characters who are fleshed out, even if they're just in three or four scenes. It makes the reader and audience feel that they're in a living, breathing universe."

If your script contains a slew of thugs, for instance, don't lump them all together and identify them by number. Give them life! Infuse them with distinct, individual qualities that stand out—and not just physically. Often writers will describe what thugs look like (one is tattooed, another scarred, another has a patch over his eye), but create nothing distinctive beyond that. They all behave the same, have the same speech pattern—they're all the same person.

Says Fandango's v.p. Cathy Rabin, "Big brownie points go to those writers who even imbue their tertiary characters with credible, complex, underlying human emotions."

Adds writer Tom Schulman, "You must force yourself to go beyond the cliches. Have that cliche flag ready to fly at any moment. If the characters are boring and cliched, we know what's coming next. We're ahead of the writer. Whereas if you as the writer can somehow surprise the audience, then you'll have characters that people are interested in watching."

Adds Susan Morgan Williams, "So often writers will pay more attention to the story and action, losing sight of the characters and their emotions. Or a lot of scripts come in and the character is one-dimensional, and to give him texture the writer will make him give up smoking. But that's not enough. The character traits have to run much deeper than that."

Sarah Pillsbury cites as a weakness "characters who are more reactive than active. They aren't forced to make tough decisions that affect their lives." This is echoed by Universal development executive Leonard Kornberg, who says "If all the protagonist is doing is reacting to what's around him rather than instigating action and propelling the story, then you have a problem. The character can't merely respond to the incidents going on around him."

"Actress/director Jennifer Warren, who's directing THE BEANS OF EGYPT, MAINE (starring Martha Plimpton and Dermot Mulroney) for American Playhouse, says, "The problem with many beginning screenwriters is that they conceive their story and fit their characters into it before they are full-blown individual people. The characters are just serving the plot, and it's not until the end that they begin to differentiate themselves as individual people. Then you have to go back and say, 'Who is this character as an individual before they're caught in a situation?'"

ESTABLISHING REAL, DIMENSIONAL CHARACTERS

So your characters must be successfully realized on the page. They must have sufficient depth, detail, clarity, believability, specificity, and individuality. The only way to create such characters is to get *inside them*, working from the inside out.

"As much as possible put yourself in the mind of the characters," says writer Darryl Ponicsan. "You must get into the depth of the character. Don't try to be clever, quick and manipulative at the sacrifice of truth. If you have a sense that it's not real, then it isn't."

Says writer Frank Pierson, "Creating dimensional characters comes down to identifying with the character: knowing who that character is, what drives them [what actors call the *spine* of the character], what their background is, their speech pattern, choice of words. You must get to know your character. You really must have a clear grasp of what that character wants in life, what he's trying to get from the other characters, how he'd behave in and react to any situation you put him in. But in many poorly written scripts, you can put your thumb over the character's name and not even know who's talking. Something is lacking there, and it's because somebody is writing with no sense of who their character is."

133

This takes us right into an examination of the character around whom your entire story revolves.

THE PROTAGONIST

What Hollywood wants in a protagonist is a unique, engaging, dynamic character with very clear, detailed, specific qualities. This character must have sufficient dimension, texture, accessibility and (depending on the demands of the genre) complexity. We must be able to empathize, identify, and in all probability, connect with him on an emotional level. We must genuinely care what happens as he is launched on a journey in pursuit of a goal. And through his struggle this character must evolve, grow and learn something through the course of the story. Is that all? No.

In the first act, we must learn as much as possible about the protagonist—who that person is physically, psychologically, emotionally and intellectually. Of course we want to discover more about the character as the script progresses, but a good writer tells us what we need to know when we need to know it. Don't make the mistake of getting so caught up in plot in the first act that we can't figure who your protagonist is.

If by page 25 or 30 we *still* don't have a firm grasp of any one character, and can't figure out whose story it is, you're in trouble. It is imperative that the main character take shape *as early as possible*.

"People will bail out at the first opportunity," says Leonard Kornberg, "and if the characters come to life in the second act but the first act stinks, it's too late. Because you haven't gotten anybody to read past the first act."

Adds Jennifer Warren, "Usually when you start reading a script, it always grabs you if a character stands out right away because he's unusual and very well drawn. If you find a character that is unusual instead of just a faceless person who slowly evolves and does not get individuated until late in the story—if ever—you're more likely to stay with the script."

In creating unusual, individual characters, the writer must probe into them.

What is his personality? Quirks, idiosyncrasies, flaws, strengths? What is engaging, interesting or even captivating about this person? Is it a star role? What is his level of morality? Honest or dishonest? What set of rules does he operate by? What is his view of the world? Where does he live and work? Where is he financially? What are his central relationships? *Be very specific!*

Have you given this character a *backstory* (past information from the character's life) before the story begins? This is a great way to learn about your character *and* create dimension.

Says Gareth Wigan, "I have for a long time been obsessed with backstory; that is, the so-called third dimension that all characters must have. It must be in some way connected to a time and place other than the story they're in. My belief is that if you spend a great deal of time figuring out who the characters are— What do they do? What did they do before the story begins? Where did they come from? Were they ever married before?— you create more dimensional characters. You don't necessarily have to put the backstory into the exposition, but it informs as it is implied in certain parts of the dialogue. Then the characters have an existence which lies behind the words they're saying, which I think makes the characters more interesting. They have a life outside the movie."

"I like ambiguity," says Joe Eszterhas. "I like to see the grays in characters. I like characters who have one front and many, many layers underneath. I like complexity; I like to surprise people with different facets of personality. I like the surprises within characters, the contradictions. I seem to be fascinated with the notion that we really don't know the people that we love, which is a theme that runs through most of my pictures— JAGGED EDGE, BETRAYED, MUSIC BOX, and BASIC INSTINCT to some extent. The idea is that we remain strangers to one another no matter how intimate we are; we really don't know the people we love past a certain point."

Says Jeb Stuart, "I like characters to have physical as well as internal struggles. I like to engage and challenge my characters on a deep, psychological and emotional level."

Adds Tom Schulman, "It seems to me that as a writer you're sort of peeling off the layers of what the character is feeling and what they want. I like to take characters who might be slightly hidden in what motivates them, what makes them tick...and then slowly show the audience what it is they want, how they get it, how they succeed or fail, and the hell they go through to get there."

So if you've been one of those writers who just skims the surface of your characters, only to find that they're dead on arrival, *you must radically change your approach.* The pros take a lot of thought, care and preparation in creating their characters. They look for ways to give them the complexities, dichotomies, levels and layers that bring them to life on the page. So you must be as probing and demanding of your characters.

What the buyers also want from most protagonists are the qualities that generate a strong *rooting interest.* If your protagonist is a hero, we want to be able to cheer that character on. In many failed scripts, however, we don't care enough that the protagonist succeeds. Either the character lacks sympathetic qualities, or there is—as we've discussed—a lack of risk or jeopardy, too little to overcome, too small a goal without enough meaning, too soft an antagonist.

But while rootability in characters is a staple of the studio mentality, writer Joe Eszterhas doesn't believe in plugging into that formula.

"I know every time you talk to an executive they talk about rootable characters, and I think that's exactly part of the problem, why you have so many really shitty movies coming out of the Hollywood system.

"I don't think you have to make characters rootable any more, in the old Hollywood sense. I think if you do that, you're playing a tired game. I'm not saying that we shouldn't care about the characters. I'm saying that we don't necessarily have to root for them or like them. If they fascinate us and interest us, then we care about them."

Referring to BASIC INSTINCT, Eszterhas says, "Neither Nick

nor Catherine are classic rootable characters, and I think we would have had some difficulty getting them through the studio system were it not for the fact that Mario [Carolco chief Mario Kassar] is a buccaneer and [director] Paul Verhoeven decided to take it right to the wall.

"Now there is a lesson here," says Eszterhas, "and I don't know if the studios will learn it. But the lesson is that if you play the old formulaic games and insist on pushing the same buttons; if you insist on what I call the 'football game' concept of movies, which is 'let's root for somebody,' then you can have a really failed, dead picture. But if you're willing to violate a lot of those rules in the '90's, I think you have a better chance of a hit picture than otherwise."

Though the importance of rootability can be debated, it is an indisputable fact that your characters must be *real*. You don't want someone to read your script and say, "Well the characters are interesting, but they just don't seem real."

To avoid this problem, writer Larry Ferguson stresses the importance of studying human behavior. "All you really need to do is study human nature. You have to get out, sit and look at people, watch the way they interact. Go to restaurants by yourself and listen to as many conversations as you can...really hear how people talk."

To imbue his characters with reality, James Toback says, "I have some kind of person in mind with each character I create. I know who they are. I watch them and listen to them."

As for Tom Schulman, "As much as possible I try to create characters who are amalgamations of people I know. I try to start with a face of someone I grew up with or met so I understand the basics of where that character is coming from. He'll probably end up in a completely fictional spot in the story, but you have to write what you know. You have to try to pin down your characters as much as possible to real people."

Darryl Ponicsan approaches character in much the same way: "I've always tried to draw a character on people I've known, and I can't make a character do something because I think it will be entertaining for the audience. I have to make sure that whatever

137

a character does is something I would do under similar circumstances or that I've seen someone else do under certain circumstances. This gives the character the ring of reality and truth."

MOVEMENT OF THE PROTAGONIST

As we discussed in Chapter 5, you must launch your protagonist on a compelling journey in which the stakes are high, the struggle fierce, and the goal of sufficient meaning and importance to both the character and the audience.

A good example of a protagonist's movement through a story can be found in the hit film HONEYMOON IN VEGAS. Written and directed by Andrew Bergman (THE IN-LAWS, THE FRESHMAN, shared writing credit on BLAZING SADDLES), HONEYMOON IN VEGAS involves Jack Singer, a New York private eye who, despite making a promise to his mother on her deathbed that he will never marry, goes to Las Vegas with his girlfriend Betsy to get hitched. But instead of walking down the aisle, a maritally phobic Jack loses $60,000 in a poker game to mobster Tommy Korman, whose late wife is a dead ringer for Betsy. And the only way Jack can pay off his huge poker debt is to "loan" Betsy to Tommy for the weekend. So begins Jack's quest to get Betsy back.

But this isn't just any quest, mind you, but a hilariously wild escapade in which a frantic Jack makes his way to Kauai, is rerouted by a cabbie on order from Tommy's sidekick, detoured by an Indian chief who sings Broadway show tunes, is attacked by Tommy, makes his way back to Vegas on a plane with Elvis impersonators, and ultimately parachutes from the plane to save Betsy from the clutches of Tommy, who plans to marry her himself.

Though it is ultimately Jack who marries Betsy, this happy moment is the culmination of his desperate *struggle* throughout the story—which is the just the point I'm trying to make here. To find Betsy and get her back, Jack must undertake the struggle of his life! In fact, he *risks his life* to get her back, becoming tougher, more determined and self-assured in the process. No longer a momma's boy, Jack becomes his own man in the end, and will now embark on a new life with Betsy.

While your protagonist may not risk his life as Jack Singer does, it is imperative that he struggle. You've got to make it tough—very tough—for your protagonist to achieve his goal. Like Jack, struggling to extract his fiancee from the clutches of a mobster, your protagonist must be fighting for something that is truly important and meaningful in his life.

MEANING & MOTIVATION

What is meaningful to the protagonist could be any number of things, depending on the feelings, attitudes, needs, and beliefs of the character. It could be another person, such as the hero rescuing a loved one in DIE HARD, or fighting against something the character vehemently believes is wrong, as in SILKWOOD. Or a character may be struggling to regain something within himself, as in THE VERDICT, in which an alcoholic attorney regains his dignity and self-respect through his pursuit of justice.

Whatever your protagonist decides is meaningful enough to fight for or against, the object of her struggle cannot be something of dubious importance to the reader. No one wants to question why a character is struggling for something, so you must make clear *why the goal is so important, what motivates the character to pursue it, how it will benefit her to achieve it, and why we should care at all that the character succeeds.*

Many scripts just bypass these critical factors and are rejected accordingly.

A common example is a protagonist who becomes a makeshift detective to solve a murder. He moves into a house once owned by the murder victim, an old photo of whom just happens to be lying in a bureau drawer. For some reason the protagonist is strangely drawn to the woman in the photo and embarks on an investigation into her death. Since he never even met the victim when she was alive, it's not clear why he even cares enough to find the killer.

What suddenly motivates him to play detective? In many scripts the motive is nonexistent, the writer failing to justify the actions of the character, or it's so flimsy that you just don't buy it. We couldn't care less if he solves the murder or that the woman was killed at all. The only way we *would* care is if she had some emotional link to the protagonist, who needs a deeper, more personal stake in what he's trying to accomplish.

Granted, movie detectives solve murders all the time without being emotionally connected to their cases. But that's what they're hired to do. That's their motivation (see discussion of murder mysteries in Chapter 7). But when a character suddenly decides to play detective for no apparent reason, when he suddenly takes a personal stake in solving the murder of a women he never knew and the motivation isn't supplied by the writer, this creates a hole you could drive a truck through.

But it isn't enough that the protagonists fiercely struggle for something that is meaningful in their lives. We must also understand the *reason* for their actions. Motivation is therefore crucial. It's wrong for the writer not to inform the reader why a character is taking a certain action; the motive must be clear. And when the motive isn't clear, it's a sure sign that a writer is externally and mechanically maneuvering their characters instead of *getting inside them*. What results is artificiality, superficiality, a lack of credibility—and more often than not, a rejected script.

Good writers will use backstory to supply motivation and justify the actions of a character.

For instance, to justify a man's desperate fear of kittens, a writer might draw from the backstory and incorporate into the script perfectly good reasons for the character's seemingly irrational behavior. Perhaps there are comical flashbacks to the man as a boy being chased down the street by hundreds of kittens. Perhaps some lines of dialogue reveal that the man has always feared kittens ever since his mother brought a vicious one home that ripped apart the couch pillows. Now these are admittedly bizarre examples, but the point is that backstory can plug holes left gaping by amateurish writers. It help justify character actions which otherwise seem questionable or unmotivated— weaknesses found in many rejected screenplays.

Says writer Gary Ross, "Backstory leads to an inevitability of events which leads to motivated behavior. Backstory should create an environment in which when the story begins, what happens to the character becomes inevitable because the preceding events in that character's life make it so.

"Willy Loman [in DEATH OF A SALESMAN] is pulled inexorably into his behavior, thus it's all motivated," Ross continues. "But the thing that drives Willy Loman isn't who he is the moment the play begins. *It's who he's been for 40 years*—going on those runs, driving that car, hawking those wares. That's been his life up to that moment. And this is all backstory; this is not anything we discover in the present in that play."

THE ARC OF THE PROTAGONIST

"I like characters to experience some kind of growth," says Andrea Asimow. "I want to see how a character evolves in the script, how I meet that character at the beginning and how he or she is tracked to the end. Does that character change somehow? Can I believe the journey? Do I relate to the journey?"

The *arc* (evolution) of the main character is of critical importance to those who read, buy, and develop scripts on a daily basis. In development meetings it is invariably discussed: How does this character arc through the story? Is the arc too soft and narrow? Is it too exaggerated? Do the character changes occur too quickly and unbelievably? Should the arc be more gradual and realistic? Are the changes too subtle, or does the character need a more sweeping arc? Does the character arc at all? If not, that usually indicates a major problem with the script.

"Arc is an overused word in our business," says Lauren Shuler-Donner," but the fact is that you have to think about yourself in the editing room and then think about yourself watching the movie. And every time this character comes on screen you want to see some sort of change. Because if the character is the same nice guy at the end of the movie as he was at the beginning, it's boring. A character definitely needs to start somewhere and then change at the end."

The change could be physical, behavioral, mental, emotional—anything to convey that the character has somehow been altered during, and as a result of, his struggle throughout the story.

The character may emerge with a completely different outlook on life, or his attitude about himself may change. The change could be a complete reversal—a character initially misanthropic ends up helping the starving people in Africa. Or a character may start out as a corrupt, greedy lawyer who, when a case he wins wipes out his father, rethinks his priorities.

Whatever it is, your protagonist should emerge with a different set of beliefs, attitudes, feelings or behavior in the end.

There are certain characters who by convention, may not arc at all—secret agents, private detectives (see Chapter 7). James Bond, for instance, is essentially the same man at the end of a story as he is at the beginning, as is detective Hercule Poirot in the Agatha Christie movies. Inspector Clouseau really doesn't change in each "Pink Panther" movie, nor does Jessica Fletcher in MURDER, SHE WROTE.

But make no mistake about it: If your story requires that the protagonist has a definite arc and exhibit a noticeable change in the end, and you don't deliver the goods—then your script will be passed on.

We also want to see that the protagonist has learned something through the course of the story. It is through this newly found knowledge that the character comes away with a different perspective about himself, life, love, or the world that he couldn't have realized without having gone on his journey.

A good example is TOOTSIE, at the end of which Michael Dorsey decides to abandon his guise as Dorothy and later tells Julie what he has learned: "I was a better man as a woman...with you, than I ever was...as a man...with a woman...if you know what I mean." He then goes on to say, "I just have to do it without the dress."

So be aware if your protagonists emerge more enlightened in some fashion by the end of the story. Did their struggles teach them anything? Do they come away with at least *something* of value because they've rethought their life? Are they now on a new and better path as a result of what they've learned? The failure of the writer to inject such elements into a script is quite often a reason for rejection and, says Amblin's Jason Hoffs, quite bluntly, "It's definitely a problem for me when a character doesn't grow, change or learn anything. I can't help but question the point of the script, and it's usually pretty boring."

THE ANTAGONIST

The plight of the protagonist is only as tough as the antagonist makes it. That is, unless the antagonist is a formidable foe, the protagonist won't struggle or suffer enough and the story will lose potency.

Like the protagonist, the antagonist must be a deftly-crafted, thoroughly developed character with the will and capacity to pursue a goal to the end. The key is that the goals of these two characters must be in direct opposition. Whatever the protagonist wants to possess or is trying to accomplish, the antagonist is struggling to prevent it with all the might he can muster. What the antagonist wants is in some way a major threat or obstacle to the protagonist, who is forced into action accordingly.

"You should have an antagonist that intrinsically throws obstacles in the protagonist's path," says writer Tom Schulman. "If it gets too easy for the protagonist, you have to rethink the antagonist. Give him better reasons to act, better motivation, draw from the backstory."

If the balance of forces is off—if the antagonist isn't in polar opposition to the protagonist or lacks the might, cunning, trickery, brute strength (whatever it takes) to thwart the protagonist—that is major problem.

Another common weakness is that there is no edge to the antagonist. If he's meant to be an out-and-out villain, he isn't dastardly, evil, sinister or fearful enough. He lacks presence; there aren't enough inventive quirks to his personality and behavior to distinguish him as unique; his scheme is too small and uneventful to pose a sufficient threat to the protagonist or the world at large. He's meant to arc or change through the story but doesn't.

This speaks to many failed screenplays, in which the problems can not only be traced to the inadequacy of the antagonist, but to the *Forces of Antagonism*: the forces at work in opposition to the protagonist. Problems include:

—The forces of antagonism are too soft and linear, failing to build in a progression

—The forces of antagonism don't continually thwart and threaten the protagonist

—The forces of antagonism don't force the protagonist to take action

—The forces of antagonism don't heighten the stakes or turn up the heat

—The forces of antagonism don't push the protagonist to the wall and force him or her to the end of the line

WHAT ABOUT BOB?

An excellent (and hilarious) illustration of an antagonist/ forces of antagonism continually thwarting a protagonist can be found in the film WHAT ABOUT BOB? Writer Tom Schulman describes the struggle of psychiatrist Dr. Leo Marvin (Richard Dreyfuss) as "the constant re-emergence of his patient Bob (Bill Murray). Each time Dr. Marvin think he's found a way to get rid of Bob, he keeps coming back. Dr. Marvin is constantly being forced to think of new, more clever and difficult ways to get rid of Bob. Even when Dr. Marvin screams 'Get out!' and slams the door, Bob is still there.

"Plus, the fact that Dr. Marvin has had a book published and is going on TV makes the stakes higher because he has more to lose. Here he is going on television, thinking he's one of the leading psychiatrists in the country, and he can't even keep this patient out of his life. It threatens Dr. Marvin's sense of who he is."

Schulman also adds a *ticking clock* device in that the TV crew is coming in the morning, giving Dr. Marvin a limited amount of time to get rid of Bob or be humiliated on live television before millions of people.

To heighten the forces of antagonism even more, Schulman aligns Bob with Dr. Marvin's family (wife, daughter, and particularly the young son), in whose eyes Bob can do no wrong.

Says Schulman, "It was essential that the family see Bob the way we see Bob: as this harmless guy who really just needs help. They're sympathetic and won't make him go away. In fact, they're part of the reason why Dr. Marvin can't get rid of him."

This makes for some hysterical scenes, particularly when Dr. Marvin nearly chokes to death and Bob saves him, the family ignoring Dr. Marvin and rallying around Bob.

What's more—*and this is critical*—Bob becomes such a formidable, unbeatable antagonist in Dr. Marvin's life that Dr. Marvin is finally pushed to what screenwriter Robert McKee calls "the end of the line." Anything less is unacceptable, because if a protagonist is only taken halfway it means that the forces of antagonism haven't been strong enough to force him to the end of the line.

Dr. Marvin ultimately has no choice but to kill Bob—but even that doesn't work! The film ends with a reversal: Dr. Marvin becomes a candidate for the loony bin, and Bob marries Dr. Marvin's sister.

Now notice the arc of both these characters. Dr. Marvin arcs from a confident successful psychiatrist to a blithering idiot in a wheelchair, though he's humbled in the process and that's what he needs. Says Schulman, "By the time the story is resolved, everybody has been tested and changed. It might have been nicer to give Dr. Marvin something more positive at the end, but the sense was that you both wanted it and you didn't. You wanted to have some satisfaction with Dr. Marvin, but anything you could think of—any happy ending for Leo Marvin—just rang false."

Bob, on the other hand, arcs from a neurotic, multiphobic mess into a functioning human being who marries his psychiatrist's sister. Says Schulman, however, "I don't think Bob ever comes to a moment of self-realization in the film, whereas I think Dr. Marvin does."

But each character does undergo some sort of change in the end, which brings us to the question of who is the protagonist and who is the antagonist. According to writer Schulman, the story is unique in that both characters exhibit the traits of protagonists, yet are antagonists in each other's lives.

"For Bob, what he wants is a family," says Schulman, "and what he gets is a family at the end. He is unconscious of that need in the beginning of the film and seems to only need help from Dr. Marvin, but as early as the first interview in Dr. Marvin's office, Bob picks up on those pictures of the family. He wants to know their names. Later he cries while watching THE BRADY BUNCH. He secretly needs to belong to a family."

Note the distinction between a character's conscious and unconscious goals, something we touched upon in Chapter 5. Bob consciously wants help from Dr. Marvin, fearing he can't function without him; but what he *really* wants deep down— what drives him throughout the story and becomes the "spine" of his character—is his desperate need for a family.

And just as Bob is the antagonist in Dr. Marvin's life, so is Dr. Marvin, Schulman notes, "the major block that Bob has in finding a family. Dr. Marvin's refusal to help him is the continuing antagonistic barb in Bob's side. At the same time, nothing Dr. Marvin does can convince Bob that he's a malevolent person. To Bob, everything Dr. Marvin does is a form of therapy —a form of love, really, in Bob's mind. So even when Dr. Marvin is trying to kill him, Bob thinks he's being helped in the form of death therapy."

But even with Dr. Marvin's antagonistic qualities, it was important to Schulman for us to perceive some good in Dr. Marvin and "not find him a truly offensive psychiatrist. He had to have a human side; he had to have an ego so we could all understand where he's coming from in terms of having this great period in his life being ruined by a patient. So in a strange way, I wrote the story as though both characters were the protagonist and the antagonist."

That's what makes WHAT ABOUT BOB? all the more intriguing. The script is an excellent example of two sharply crafted characters—each in pursuit of something in his own life while throwing obstacles in the path of the other.

So in the writing of your script, always question whether the forces acting upon your protagonist are strong enough. Because it is through the antagonistic forces that conflict is injected into a script, momentum builds, the protagonist is plunged deeper and deeper into trouble.

HOW DO CHARACTERS REVEAL THEMSELVES?

A sure sign of an amateur is when characters are primarily revealed through dialogue instead of action and behavior. Just as talkiness is a structural problem and a sign of overwritten dialogue (see Chapters 5 and 8), it is also an indication that the writer isn't revealing the true nature of the characters.

Though dialogue can reveal character, it is limiting. We learn infinitely more about a character by what he does.

Explains Jennifer Warren, "In the theater you have to rely on the words because you can't get that close to the person to really see what they're not saying. It's a very verbal medium, which film is not. Because in a film the actor can say so much by being silent. The camera looks at you and is close enough that the audience can read what you're thinking...what you're not saying. And most of the things that we don't say in our lives are probably more interesting than what we do say. We automatically edit everything that we say depending on where we are, who we're talking to, what we're talking about, and if you can see what the person is editing by what they're not saying, it says a lot about who they are. But many screenwriters make the mistake of over-explaining their characters."

Adds Gareth Wigan, "Often writers fall back on describing a character, and if you stripped the description out, you find there really isn't enough actual character there. The writers don't know how to establish a character, and even tend to fall back on describing what a character is thinking."

The Kevin Costner film REVENGE contains a strong example of a character revealed by behavior. When we first meet the Anthony Quinn character, he's a seemingly warm, generous, gracious man, entertaining friends in the back yard of his elegant home. The mood is light and comfortable—until Quinn catches his Rotweiler playfully wrestling with a leather jacket on the lawn. It is here that the true nature of Quinn's character bursts forth as he violently picks the dog up by the skin and smashes it into the swimming pool. These two pieces of behavior immediately tell us that this man is wildly intolerant, controlling and above all—violent.

Had we merely been *told* about the character's violent nature, it wouldn't have had the impact. We must see a character in action to fully understand who he is *inside*.

Universal story analyst Michael Serafin explains how in the film BULLITT, "Steve McQueen goes to the store to buy frozen dinners, and all he does is go right down the frozen row and throw things in his cart. He doesn't care what the dinners are; he just needs food for the week. And his indifference, in that one little gesture, made me understand more about him than 20 pages of him addressing a fellow cop saying, 'God, I'm really indifferent.'"

Characters are also revealed by the choices they make (or choose not to make) in the presence of conflict. The greater the conflict and the more demanding the choice, the more revealing of character. When a character is forced to make an excruciating decision amidst tremendous conflict, then the deepest quality of character is displayed.

In many failed screenplays, however, the characters mostly talk mostly about themselves or are perfunctorily revealed by other characters. Their actions say little or nothing about who they are. Their behavior isn't indicative of any particular type of character or is out of character. They aren't forced into behavior that reveals their inner core. The result: The reader can't get a handle on who the characters are.

As summed up by Jennifer Warren: "Film is about revealing characters through behavior, and behavior is the best teller of character in a film."

CONSISTENCY

Finally, it is important that your characters be consistent. After you have imbued them with texture, complexity, individuality and reality, your characters must consistently speak and behave "in character."

Says New Regency Productions president Steven Reuther, "I look for consistency in characters. Is each character differentiated from the other and is their behavior consistent? Do they have a particular way of speaking that is consistent? In some scripts, one character's lines could be traded with another character's and you wouldn't know the difference."

On the other hand, there may be little inconsistencies in characters that make them more intriguing, less predictable.

Says Jennifer Warren, "The moment you know exactly what a character is going to do, why continue reading the rest of the script? But if the characters are so individual that you're never quite sure, that's intriguing. Now what character would you not think would get into this situation? Oh, I could never imagine Aunt Lucy being the one who goes in and saves the child from the lake."

So by all means make your characters consistent enough to be clear and credible. Give them a manner of speaking and behaving that is specifically indicative of who they are.

Then go a step further; bend your characters in ways we wouldn't expect. Create interesting dichotomies so the characters aren't completely on the nose. Have them take certain actions we're surprised by, or throw them into situations they wouldn't normally be in. That makes the difference between a character who is blandly consistent and one who entertainingly throws us for a loop.

Says Jennifer Warren, "The unexpected is always worth investigating."

A RECAP:

—Plot and character are inextricably linked, each continually influencing the other

—The industry wants characters who are: castable, unique, powerful, dimensional, fleshed out, motivated, clear, real, consistent yet unpredictable, textured, complex, idiosyncratic, sympathetic and worth rooting for and caring about

—Avoid characters who are: stereotypical, cliched, one-dimensional, mechanical, artificial, superficial, boring, on the nose, blatantly predictable, vastly inconsistent, impossible to figure out, simplistic, emotionally void, hollow, too reactive

—Create characters from the inside out. Learn everything you can about them psychologically, emotionally, intellectually. Give them a backstory

—Imbue even your secondary and tertiary characters with dimension and individuality

—Time the entrance of your characters properly, and establish the protagonist very early on

—Develop an arc for your characters: Do they grow, change, and learn throughout the story?

—The protagonist must have a personal stake in what s/he is struggling to achieve. The struggle must have meaning

—The antagonist or forces of antagonism, must have the capacity to continually thwart the protagonist

—Characters should primarily be revealed through behavior, not dialogue.

7

Genre

The success of many screenplays hinges on whether the structure is appropriate to the genre, and whether the writer has successfully adhered to certain genre conventions.

An action script will fail, for example, if primarily driven by talk. A romance is doomed if we don't have an emotional investment in the lovers' third-act reconciliation. The mark of a good thriller is a wealth of tension and suspense.

Genre is also an important consideration to the buyers in terms of development. Says Paramount's Margaret French, "We have a meeting with the story analysts once a month to let them know what the studio is looking for in particular, whether it's comedy, drama, thriller, action-adventure—wherever we feel we're light in our development slate."

So if word goes out that Paramount is looking for a psychological thriller, Universal wants a children's comedy, Disney's ready to reel in a mother-daughter drama and Warner Bros. is on the lookout for an action-adventure—ideally one of your scripts will fit the bill.

Few screenplays fall squarely into only one genre. Many are a mix of genres—comedy, romance, mystery, action—the writer juggling several at a time, though it is rare that all are successfully executed. A script may be funny, but the romance is sort of trite and the mystery too convoluted.   Or a sci-fi comedy may present a visually intriguing world of the future filled with wild creatures and flashy gadgetry, but there's no story and the comedy falls flat.

So a lot depends on the writer's ability to successfully execute and blend one or more genres. In this chapter we'll examine six genres and get it straight from the masters' mouths.

COMEDY

This may sound painfully obvious, but judging from how many unsuccessful comedies are submitted to studios and production companies every day, it needs to be said: *A COMEDY NEEDS TO BE FUNNY!*

If it's not funny, what good is it?

Moreover, an uproariously funny comedy can often tolerate more weaknesses than any other genre. The plotting can bit a obvious and predictable, which would spell death to a murder mystery. The characters need not have the depth and inner dimension of, say, a dramatic character study. Cliches can be poked fun at and made hilarious, whereas they're awful and unintentionally laughable in a police drama.

With that said, it is indeed perplexing why a writer *without* an innate feel for comedy would choose this genre over all others. Why write comedy if you don't naturally think funny? Some people can't tell a joke to save their lives.

This is why comedy is such a prickly genre for many writers.

Says executive Michael Schulman, "When I council writers, I say if you can write comedy, great. That's exactly what you should be because there are very few people who can do it well. But in terms of trying to begin a career and really trying to get somewhere, comedy—more so than any other genre—is something that either hits or misses. There's no gray area. If you're writing a thriller, somebody might say, `Well, this kind of didn't work in the third act, but there's some really good writing here'—or—'this is a good character. Why don't I bring this person in and maybe we can work on it?' But if a comedy just doesn't work, it's all over. This is particularly true of high concept/broad comedy."

On the other hand, a wild and wacky parody that pulls out all the stops and never lets up can bring you all the success you've dreamed of. Case in point: POLICE ACADEMY.

Says production executive Gareth Wigan, "I have spoken in the past about a period in my life where I overlapped working on two movies. One was THE RIGHT STUFF, which may certainly be one of the very best movies I've been involved with. I was also working on a movie called POLICE ACADEMY, which I enjoyed as well. One was a great movie but not a financial success; the other was less than a great movie and spawned an empire."

Looking beyond the obvious fact that a comedy must make people laugh, what makes a comic screenplay—farce, slapstick, screwball, satire, black comedy—fly?

I remember reading HONEYMOON IN VEGAS and laughing out loud for most of the script. Even the off-camera directions were funny, so innately comedic is writer Andrew Bergman. And if a screenplay is so funny it makes you laugh out loud, there's a good chance it's going to get some attention.

Says executive Andrea Asimow, "If a high-concept comedy comes across my desk and I find myself laughing, which is rare, then I can't help but pay very close attention to it. Simply because I sat there reading it and had a good time, then I'm going to be pretty enthusiastic about it."

Now how you approach a comedy obviously depends on what type you're dealing with. But let's say you're going for an off-the-wall, wacky comedy along the lines of POLICE ACADEMY, AIRPLANE!, THE NAKED GUN, YOUNG FRANKENSTEIN, BLAZING SADDLES or HOT SHOTS.

The mistake many writers make is that they don't take the humor all the way to the wall. They don't go to extremes and pull out all the stops, but stay too close to the middle. Instead of the gut-busting laughs that would have audiences rolling in the aisles, they only elicit smiles and chuckles. Either the writers are unable to come up with the really funny laughs or seem inhibited and afraid of going too far.

Better to go too far and have to pull back later than to not go far enough. If you're too tame you undermine the comedy. You've got to go all out.

Remember in AIRPLANE! when the little girl says to the stewardess that she prefers her coffee black, just like her men? Or when Peter Graves asks the boy if he's ever seen a grown man naked? Or when Julie Hagerty gives a blow job to an inflatable doll? Remember in YOUNG FRANKENSTEIN when the horses whinny every time the name "Frau Blucher" is mentioned? Or when the blind man hears the monster growl and says, "Oh, you're a mute...an incredibly big mute." Or when Dr. Frankenstein notes the knockers on the castle door and his assistant Inga thanks him, assuming he's referring to her breasts?

This is just the kind of hilariously extreme humor that a laugh-a-minute comedy must have to succeed.

Which brings up another common problem: many writers don't time their comedies properly. They'll go too long without a laugh; the jokes are too sporadically placed. Something might be funny on page 10, and it isn't until page 25 that the comedy resurfaces. You can't help but say in the course of reading these scripts, "And this is supposed to be a comedy?! Why are the laughs spread so damn thin?!"

Says Pat Proft (co-writer of POLICE ACADEMY, THE NAKED GUN: FROM THE FILES OF POLICE SQUAD, NAKED GUN 2/12, HOT SHOTS), "The idea is to put in as many jokes as you can possibly get into a frame. You go from gag to gag to gag, and the jokes have to be extremely good. You try to get as many jokes in on every page."

In writing a parody, then, you must be aware if it's been too long since the last laugh. You can't go 10, 15, 20 pages in a rapid-fire spoof without something funny happening or being said. The laughs have got to come thick and fast, and the comedy must be wildly inventive and razor sharp, both verbally and visually.

This type of comedy must also contain a logical, well-structured story on which to hang the jokes.

Says Proft, "We do spend an awful long time coming up with a story that seems plausible. So if you just read the story, it would seem like it belongs in a dramatic film. The story has a dramatic base because you're trying to do the type of serious movies you're parodying. For instance, the first NAKED GUN was about somebody trying to kill the Queen of England. The story has to sound serious before the jokes go in."

Moreover, it's important that the jokes fit the characters and situation.

"A lot of times," Proft continues, "a joke or whole sequences have to come out, even though they're funny, because they just don't fit. You can't force the comedy. In NAKED GUN 2 1/2, a very funny prison scene had to come out because it stopped the film just to do prison jokes. It interrupted the flow of the story rather than following a natural arc. So it had to come out. Now the upcoming NAKED GUN 3 is built around that scene, and by starting from there, now it makes sense."

Another integral ingredient is a cast of absolutely hysterical characters. From their physical characteristics to their behavior, from the words they say to their distinct manner of speaking, each and every character must in some way enhance the comedy. Some are played straight, as with the Lloyd Bridges' character in AIRPLANE! Others are played to the hilt, as with the Madeline Kahn and Cloris Leachman characters in YOUNG FRANKEN-STEIN. The only rule is that they have to be funny.

Examine the hit parodies and outrageous comedies. Notice how broad and extreme the comedy is, writers refusing to flounder around the middle. Notice how the laughs just pour out of those films one after another, how the humor stems from every source imaginable: dialogue, sight gags, characters, physical comedy, plot turns. The writers pull every lever, and we're in stitches throughout.

On the other hand, some comedies are more reality-based. As Lowell Ganz (co-writer with Babaloo Mandel) explains, the emphasis isn't so much on being consistently funny as it is on keeping the audience hooked.

"Once we've written the script and we read it to ourselves, it has to what we call 'pay its own way.' It has to be interesting, exciting, funny, moving, emotional. It has to be anything other than boring. That's the only rule. We won't necessarily say we've gone too long without a comic scene, but we'll question: Why are we dull here? What have we done wrong? What is not working here? Why are these five pages boring?"

Ganz and Mandel also avoid what is known as one-liner comedy, and instead allow the humor to come from the characters and the situation.

With a handful of notable exceptions such as CHEERS, MURPHY BROWN, SEINFELD, ROSEANNE and EVENING SHADE, the bulk of TV sitcoms are one-liner comedy. There's a setup, the joke, and then the laugh track (without which there would often be dead silence). For feature films, however, audiences expect more than that. They don't want to get in their car, drive to the theater, plop down seven bucks and see the same thing they could have seen in their own living room.

Yet that is exactly what many failed screenplays offer. They're merely glorified sitcoms, the writer hinging all the humor on a series of stale, crass, decidedly unfunny one-liners. The characters and plot turns aren't amusing, and if you stripped away all the incessantly jokey dialogue, there wouldn't be any comedy left.

The better writers approach it differently.

Says Lowell Ganz, "We'll write a scene that we think is pretty good, and afterwards somebody—the director, star, producer—has come up with a great joke out of context that they'd like us to put in. Now we take the scene back and start to read it, and we're having a tremendous amount of trouble getting another line in. Well, that's great. That's a good thing. Because the scene is tight, it's natural. Each line is a natural outgrowth of the previous line; it's conversational. And it becomes very, very hard to get another line into the scene. I always feel very good when that happens."

Adds writer Leslie Dixon, "I almost never think in terms of one-liners. I try to make the comedy come out of the situation. Once in a while I'll go back over a flat scene and add some verbal humor, and that's usually the most forced and shittiest writing that I do."

It's impossible to write a very real, very human comedy solely from the standpoint of yuk-yuk dialogue. Though funny dialogue has to be there, undue emphasis on it at the expense of the characters and story will invariably yield phony, forced, mechanical writing.

"We work very hard on character, plot and structure," says Ganz. "We never approach it from the standpoint of what would be funny. The key for us initially is the characters. From that point on, we're never trying to think of what would be a funny line. It always has to follow out of the characters and their behavior—what they need and want.

"When I first started working in TV 20 years ago, I used to work on THE ODD COUPLE series and Jack Klugman taught me a great lesson. He would always ask me: What do I want in this scene? Well, because I was fresh out of college and didn't know any better, I thought he wanted good jokes. But he would explain to me that the character walks into a room and what is his intention? What is his agenda? What is he hoping will happen in the next five minutes? And I think that is very much at the core of everything we try to do."

Using PARENTHOOD as an example, Ganz explains, "There's a scene near the end of the movie when Steve Martin is sort of wallowing in his depression, and he gets into an argument with his wife (Mary Steenburgen) about something his grandmother told him. The wife agrees with the grandmother and starts yelling at her husband, telling him what a depressed, negative person he is, and that she thinks his grandmother is a brilliant woman.

"At that point Steve Martin looks outside and says, 'If she's so brilliant, why is she sitting in our neighbor's car?' This always gets a great laugh, and the joke comes out of character. He wants to get the last word; he's frustrated. It's the sort of thing he would say because he's down on everything at this point. Those kinds of laughs, to me, are the ideal laughs, rather than machine-gunning. You always have to give every character in every scene an attitude. That's what's crucial. When you see bad TV, the jokes aren't so much coming out of an understandable attitude, unless the attitude could be called I make a joke at everything the other person says."

So with a reality-based comedy the writer must walk a fine line between keeping the writing honest and not allowing the comedy to disappear completely. The laughs still have to be there, but must be more than just a series of jokes.

"If you asked people what they liked about CITY SLICKERS," says Ganz, "most would say, quite naturally, quite understandably, that it's funny. It's got good jokes. And I agree with them; that is what's there. But the work that is done to build the foundation has allowed them to make those judgments. It has allowed them to find the movie funny and entertaining."

ACTION

What is the difference between a B-level actioner that goes straight to video after a disastrous opening weekend and such mega-hits as DIE HARD and LETHAL WEAPON? It isn't that the hits have more action. Quite often the main difference is *character*.

Says development v.p. Susan Morgan Williams, "LETHAL WEAPON is a brilliant example of an extremely well-written script with very complex yet easy to understand characters. The Mel Gibson, character, not caring whether he lives or dies because he's given up on life, really sets the stage for an incredible character. And the dichotomy is Danny Glover's character, who's life is sort of coming to an end but not of his choice. So there's a great balance between the two of them."

Adds Imagine's Bennett Schneir, "It's really the characters who pull off LETHAL WEAPON. People went to see LETHAL WEAPON 3 not because they think there's going to a great plot. They want to see those guys again. If you have an action picture with one action scene after another but the characters are nothing, forget it. Action pictures are among the most character-driven in existence. Most writers don't realize that and think it's the action. I've read scripts containing 10-page car chases and five-page shoot-outs, but there's nothing else there."

I recently passed on an action script, and the attached cover letter from the agent said, "Because this is meant to be a low-budget film, you'll find that there is more emphasis on action than character development." And I immediately thought, "*What?*" Have strong, well-defined characters suddenly become more expensive to shoot? Is an oil refinery explosion somehow less economical than a great hero and villain?

What in the world was that agent talking about? The reason the script wasn't worth pursuing was that the characters were vacuous and undeveloped. And without substantive characters with at least a little edge, all you get is empty action.

The story centers on a man living on the edge and taking too many nips from the bottle. He's struggling to make it as a writer and, like the Riggs character in LETHAL WEAPON, is living out of a trailer. So already the script is derivative. What's more, just like the hero in DIE HARD, the man is estranged from his wife and two kids. By now I'm thinking to myself, "Is there anything about this script that is original?" Well, no. It isn't long before the wife and kids are kidnapped by a band of psychos, and what ensues is essentially a road actioner in which the man trails the psychos across the state to rescue his family.

The writer had ripped off the character elements in a couple of multimillion dollar hits, and done it ineptly. We don't care about anyone. We don't feel the love between the man and his family, the script lacking a strong emotional undercurrent. Not so, however, in DIE HARD.

Says Matt Taybak, former vice president of development for Silver Pictures, (Joel Silver produced, with Larry Gordon, DIE HARD): "One of the reasons DIE HARD works so well is there's an emotional core or spine to the movie. Between the great action sequences and the concept of this guy being stuck alone in this building and have to fend off the villains, he's also

estranged from his wife. The two of them have already had a little spat when he came back to see her, yet they realize they're in
love while all the action is going on. It's also set against the
backdrop of Christmastime, so you get the sense of family values. Now I'm not saying that that is what the movie is about; it's
not. But it's laced throughout, and it's the difference between a
good and great movie for the genre."

The script I passed on was also about family. But DIE HARD
had emotional depth, whereas the rejected script was merely a
platform for violent action. It lacked a human element, the characters reduced to stick figures amidst shoot-outs, car chases,
explosions. Moreover, the characters in the script weren't firmly
established before the action kicked in, so you never come to
know them well enough to care whether they live or died.

In DIE HARD, writers Jeb Stuart and Steven E. de Souza created
a fully dimensional, emotionally involving hero in John McClane
(Bruce Willis), who isn't launched into action until about 30 pages
in. "He spends the first 30 minutes trying to call the police," says
de Souza, "which tells you a lot about who this man is. He does
everything he can to get the police to come, and when they do
come and can't solve the problem, he has no choice."

This reluctance on McClane's part is a major element in his
character. It makes him more real, more human.

Says de Souza, "I think in real life people are scared and reluctant, and that always makes the best hero for me. At the beginning of the movie, McClane is a New York cop on vacation. He
doesn't have an assignment. No one says we want you to go in
the building and rescue people. He's just minding his own business. And the fact that he wasn't a shoot-'em-up hero made him
more interesting. The reality that somebody who sees 12 men
with machine guns would run and hide was a novelty. But it
worked for the audience and now people are looking for that."

In the original LETHAL WEAPON, writer Shane Black
devotes at least the first thirty minutes to the introduction of
Riggs and Murtaugh, both Vietnam vets. Great care is taken in
depicting Riggs as a suicidal, wildly unpredictable cop who's

been emotionally torn apart by the death of his wife, and Murtaugh as veteran cop and family man who's just celebrated his 50th birthday. By the end of the first act we have a very strong handle on who these men are. They become the spine of the movie. The meticulous attention to character and the evolving relationship between Riggs and Murtaugh makes the script about much more than just action. It has depth and resonance, wit and humor. We're entertained, and care about the characters.

Universality is another critical ingredient in an action hero, and all the great ones possess it. They are typically fighting for some universal truth such as freedom, patriotism, justice, love, or family, against what is universally accepted as evil.

Even the anti-heroes (savage warriors who operate outside the laws and codes of society) have a universality; they are fighting for the moral good.

In RAMBO: FIRST BLOOD, PART II, he returns to the Vietnam prison camp from which he escaped to rescue American MIAs. The film is awash in pro-American, anti-Communist ideology as the jingoistic Rambo, a one-many army with only a knife, a bow and arrows, seeks revenge against his enemies.

A Communist enemy is at the center of ROCKY IV, in which Rocky takes on Drago, a giant of a Soviet fighter who's pumped with steroids and trains on the most technologically advanced equipment. But where Drago represents the cold, steely "evil empire," Rocky epitomizes the American hero who believes in a strong work ethic and trains like a naturalist: trudging through the frozen tundras of the Soviet Union, lifting huge piles of stones, and pulling oxcarts.

Said *Newsweek* magazine (12/23/85) of Rocky, "... he knocked the rust off the whole canon of traditional American values and became their exemplar. He loved his family. He was loyal to his friends. He was kind to animals. He believed in the American Dream of opportunity for all, and achieved it by hard, unremitting labor. He raised the work ethic to a nearly religious plane; his training for his fights became a saintly mortification of the flesh, a rite of purification requiring his retreat to various wildernesses—a meat-packing plant, a hostile ghetto gym and finally, in "Rocky IV," the frozen steppes of Russia."

Rambo, said *Newsweek*, "...was a hero—a kind of noble savage who got fed up with the system that reduces men to numbers and who took arms against it with wit, cunning and skill."

Rambo was a symbol of freedom and retribution to the masses, whose private rage was vicariously released through his violence. Outside of the movie, people who actually carry out their violent fantasies are viewed as insane. You hear in the news about a postal worker venting his frustrations in a violent manner; he's considered some lunatic who's gone crazy with a gun. You hear about someone taking shots at the president and he's immediately carted away.

But *inside* the movie, Rambo is both violent and heroic. He can kill and get away with it. And that, one suspects, is at the core of his success as a character. Said *Newsweek*, "His rage is meant to be cathartic, for himself and, Stallone guesses, for all those guys out there with their own wars to fight."

One-man army heroes, despite their violent natures, are also tremendously rootable characters, because they typically don't just kill for the hell of it and aren't driven by evil. Some even garner our sympathy.

In PREDATOR, Dutch (Arnold Schwarzenegger), the leader of a military rescue team, actually sheds a tear before gunning down a guerilla unit in a foiled rescue attempt. So Dutch is a killer, yes, but one with a conscience. You feel for the guy because he truly feels badly about what he's doing. In fact, he won't even view himself as a killer, and at one point says, "We're a rescue team, not assassins." Dutch's guilty conscience makes him human, sympathetic, and identifiable.

Now what about the villains? In poor action scripts they're thin and cliched, therefore not genuinely frightening. There isn't enough depth, style, and definition, and they simply come off as run-of-the-mill bad guys doing bad things. They don't infuse the script with their own brand of evil, and whatever means they use to foil the hero don't seem strong or sinister enough.

Says Steven de Souza, "One of the most important elements in an action picture is that the hero and villain be equal and that the hero is something of an underdog. But you see a lot of movies that don't work because it's no contest for the hero, and the villain is just your ordinary thug who may be a little bit psychotic. And there's just no balance there. So even though the audience knows that the actor they recognize playing the lead is going to survive at the end, you still want to create some doubt. You must have that balance—and when in doubt, you give the upper hand to the villain, not the hero."

Says Matt Tabak, "The less interesting the villain, the less interesting the hero. I beat my head against the wall all day long trying to come up with good villains and good plots as to what the bad guys could be doing. I mean, if you're talking about Arab terrorists, who cares? You talk to me about trafficking drugs, who cares? These things have been done ten billion times in movies and TV. But the villain in DIE HARD was different. He was smart, intelligent. And you might say that he was only after money, but greed is a great motivator. Greed is something everyone can understand."

In creating a villain, the question is whether to go for brutal realism, or to inject some humor and even make the character a bit cartoonish. Obviously, if you're doing something like BATMAN, the villains must be cartoonish, just as they are in the James Bond pictures. And DIE HARD's villain ("Hans Gruber") has a lot of wit and humor, which is evident in many of his exchanges with McClane. But there is one thing that Gruber is *not*: a caricature.

Says De Souza, "I've always tried to create villains who are a little more believable. The villains in the Bond pictures are the ones who chew the scenery and talk about throwing people to piranhas. But the pictures have been in decline for a number of years, which may indicate that audiences aren't as willing to buy those villains anymore.

"In DIE HARD the villain comes in and says if everyone will cooperate, no one will be hurt. He's very civil and polite. And of course he gradually begins to unravel and becomes more violent. But he makes a very civilized entrance."

Indeed, Gruber has a certain depth and style that makes him strangely alluring. He even speaks eloquently, saying to a group of people at the company Christmas party after killing their boss, "Your Mr. Takagi, alas, will not be joining us for the rest of his life."

"I mean, look at Kadafi in his interview with Barbara Walters," says de Souza. "He didn't say I want to destroy civilization as we know it. He said we're a small country, we're being picked on...we're the victim here."

It is also important that the twisted logic of the villains seem perfectly right and logical *from their perspective*. In other words, the Hitlers, Jeffrey Dahmers and Charlie Mansons of the world don't think like the average person off the street, that killing is wrong and there are consequences to their actions. If you polled a group of psycho killers, they're not going to say how awful they are to have committed such atrocities. In their minds, they simply did what had to be done.

Adds writer Larry Ferguson, "I believe that the nature of evil is seductive, and if you want to get away from a cartoon villain and write about people as they really are, you have to understand that nobody considers themselves to be evil or bad from their point of view. So you have to put yourself in that point of view. If a corrupt cop moves to arrest a bad guy, the cartoon way is that there's a big gun fight. But you can move over to the other side and put yourself in the skin of the person who sees the badge, and that's betrayal. That's real."

So to give your villains life on the page beyond a stereotype, infuse them with an internal logic all their own. *Why* is this person doing these awful things? What legitimizes their behavior from their point of view?

"To me a bad movie is one in which the villain is doing crazy things, but it's not explained why he does anything," says de Souza. "So the idea is to create a villain who has a clear agenda, who works carefully, who is insidious—not just randomly violent and shooting somebody for no reason at all. I never buy into that."

I've read many scripts in which you can't figure out why the villain is killing people or what he wants. Or you understand the reason but it's too flimsy to believed. Or the writer withholds the villain's motivation until late in the second act, then in three pages spills out an overly detailed, wordy, convoluted explanation to justify the villain's actions. This is particularly deadly in an action script, when the writer stops the momentum cold for an utterly boring spillage of dialogue. What's worse, there is suddenly so much information to assimilate that the reader has to go back through the script to figure out what the writer is talking about.

Villains are that much more sinister when their goal not only puts the hero at tremendous risk, but also the community or world at large. So what begins as an isolated problem has a ripple effect that may ultimately have disastrous effects for the entire nation. A common problem with many villains is that what they seek to accomplish is too small and contained, the danger too limiting and narrow to be truly frightening.

Another problem is exceedingly profane dialogue in an action script. If you recall, neither DIE HARD nor LETHAL WEAPON contain a lot of crude, vulgar language, which only tends to cheapen the genre, pandering to the lowest common denominator. But I've read and personally passed on a lot of trashy action scripts whose writers have a penchant for dialogue like, "Fuck you, you dirty cunt whore! Fuck you, you asshole bastard!" Some awful action scripts are literally filled to the brim with that kind of talk and, to my mind, that is not what the genre is about. A villain isn't any more frightening because he says the word "Fuck" every five seconds. My advice is to keep the profanity to a minimum or leave it out entirely. It's always better to write a stylish, inventive actioner than one which relies on gutter dialogue.

As for the premise and story, a straightforward actioner need not contain an intricately detailed, complex story line. It must be compelling, plunging the hero into a life-threatening situation against a thoroughly despicable villain you love to hate. And it definitely helps to inject wit and humor into the mix, both visually and verbally. But most hit action pictures have fairly simple but sturdy lines. In fact, depending on the piece, too much narrative complexity could conceivably diminish the drive.

Though the thriller-actioner THE HUNT FOR RED OCTOBER was enormously successful on screen, writer Larry Ferguson says, "You could get up for popcorn in the middle of the hunt, miss ten minutes, and really not be able to figure out what's going on." But thrillers are typically more plot-driven than straight action pictures, whose main ingredients are characters, inventive, gripping action and, quite often, special effects.

As for "buddy action" pictures, so many have come and gone that the genre is nearly exhausted. It's going to take a spectacular premise for yet another buddy cop picture to fly, the buying community admittedly bored by that genre at the time of this writing (LETHAL WEAPON notwithstanding). So unless you have what seems to be the next major blockbuster, it's probably wise to steer clear of "buddy action" premises until the buyers are more receptive.

A good action premise offers a fresh take on the genre, not a blatant rehash. Come up with a situation that hasn't been before, or perhaps a vaguely familiar situation with a distinct twist. There should also be some uniqueness to the heroes and villains that is readily apparent in a log line. You must force yourself to go beyond cliche and make your premise stand out. Because if an executive reads it in a log line and isn't interested, you're out of there before he even reads the script.

Finally, an action script must MOVE. It cannot be driven by talk, as is often the problem. The momentum must build like wildfire. It cannot be bogged down by description. A good action movie builds, builds, builds with tension, suspense and excitement galore.

Says Universal Picture's story analyst Michael Serafin, "What made LETHAL WEAPON special is that Shane Black had a very terse way of writing, almost limiting the description to a few choice words. But the images that came from them would spring off the page. I knew exactly what they could potentially look like on screen. But in a lot of cases, writers tend to overwrite to convince you they have it all worked out, and it gets to be very pedestrian reading a bullet cross the room and go right through somebody's head. You get the idea in a second; you don't need 23 lines to show that."

I've read scripts that work when guns are blazing and bombs are going off, falling flat in every other respect. In such cases the action becomes the story because there is nothing else beyond that. Many writers assume that if they fill their scripts with action-filled episodes there will be sufficient drive and emotional involvement. Wrong! You can't just haphazardly throw tons of action in. The action has to *mean something*.

In DIE HARD, Jeb Stuart says that he and Steven de Souza "tied the story into the action sequences to bring more meaning to the action. The action in a film may be terrific, but it doesn't really propel the story or tell us anything to get us to the next scene. Putting meaningful plot turns in the action alleviates that problem."

Adds de Souza, "I have never found myself in a situation where I have created a generic action scene—your generic car chase or fist fight. I try to have the action be part of the setting of the movie, which I think creates a hyper-reality that's very plausible.

"In Hitchcock's THE MAN WHO KNEW TOO MUCH, there were mysterioso events which took place in Switzerland. There was a secret message written inside of a chocolate wrapper, and danger on the ski slopes. It was New Year's Eve and someone was shot, but the sound was muffled by the popping of champagne bottles. That creates a sense of the action being an honest outgrowth of the setting and situation. In DIE HARD, things happened involving stairwells, elevators, unfinished office equipment—which made the action specific to the setting of this particular movie."

In mediocre action scripts, however, the action could take place anywhere and is generally contrived. You can see the writer's machinations: throw in a car chase and shoot-out here, explosion there. It's just random, meaningless action which isn't tied to either the setting or the heart of the characters.

And as for the action itself, do your damndest to think of something NEW! How many times have you seen the villain killed at the end by plummeting over an embankment or grabbing onto a loose wire and getting electrocuted? How many times have you seen the climactic fight between hero and villain take place on a catwalk? How many times have you seen the villain ultimately impaled on a shard of glass? We've all seen this a hundred times, and it's your job to buck the obvious. Remember that classic scene in RAIDERS OF THE LOST ARK when a bad guy is coming at Indy with a knife and Indy shoots him? The audience howled because it was so clever, so witty.

Also keep in mind that not all action pictures require ammunition and hardware from start to finish. Again, the better writer transcends the formula. Says de Souza, "I always try to have my characters lose their guns or run out of ammunition and have a more visceral hand-to-hand combat. If you look at DIE HARD, you see that for such a heavily armed group of people, there's an awful lot of bare-knuckle combat because it's much more interesting."

When an action writer virtually resurrects the genre, as Shane Black did with LETHAL WEAPON, that generates a lot of heat in the industry and at the box office. But a typical actioner with generic chases, shoot-outs and bad guys will get lost in the shuffle. You've got to go beyond that. If you want a script that stands above the rest, you must breathe as much new life and excitement into the genre as you can.

THRILLERS

Like THE SILENCE OF THE LAMBS, or Alfred Hitchcock's REAR WINDOW, STRANGERS ON A TRAIN, SPELLBOUND, NOTORIOUS and VERTIGO, a successful thriller is driven by taut, edge-of-your seat suspense and a thoroughly gripping plot line that builds like a roller coaster. Shock value is a major factor, as is a strong sense of jeopardy for the protagonist, whose predicament becomes increasingly terrifying and seemingly undefeatable.

Unfortunately, many writers don't have a handle on this genre, and their thrillers are passed on accordingly.

As you might expect, problems include a distinct *lack* of genuine suspense and mounting tension. The plotting ranges from thin, limp and obvious to convoluted, unbelievable and riddled with holes.

Because you're often dealing with implausible situations, gaping holes can kill a thriller—such as a woman entering a room where the killer is instead of phoning the police. The writer must give ample reason why all the lights are off in the house, why the woman can't get to the phone, why she can't run out of the house, why she doesn't hide in a closet. You've got to keep the tension thick by having the woman and killer come together, but you've got to plug all the holes and tell us why, creating white-knuckle terror instead of disbelief.

Says writer Nicholas Meyer, who worked on FATAL ATTRACTION, and wrote and directed the time travel thriller TIME AFTER TIME (H.G. Wells vs. Jack the Ripper in modern day San Francisco), "What is often missing in thrillers is believability. We all want to show scenes that thrill, but how do you make them believable? So the trick is to deliver your thrills within the context of a plausible reality. It's when the reality becomes implausible and the manipulation is exposed that audiences get angry. The response to failed thrillers is usually the contemptuous response that people give when they've seen through the devices."

Adds Jeb Stuart, "You have to close all the doors [plug the holes], and the more skillfully those doors are closed, the better the thriller."

Other problems include a lack of twists, turns, shocks and surprise. If the writer fails to reverse expectation, the story falls flat. It's too easy to anticipate events from scene to scene, and predictability sets in. Due to a lack of real danger and genuine terror, the protagonist is never in enough jeopardy to warrant our cogent concern... *PASS.*

Tom Holland wrote PSYCHO 2, directed and co-wrote CHILD'S PLAY, and just finished directing THE TEMP for Paramount, a "psychological thriller with erotic overtones" about a "killer" temp secretary. He says, "Terror doesn't work on what you see. It works on what you don't see. It works on anticipation. What you want is to constantly reverse the audience's expectations by making them think something is going to happen, then not having it happen and then they turn around and it does happen. A successful thriller is build on this kind of anticipation."

To heighten the terror and suspense, Holland says, "Create the most terrifying villain you can, which means overwhelming odds. How is your hero ever going to win? From the get-go, there is no fucking way that your hero is ever going to survive this. That makes the heights to which your hero must rise that much greater. Things must constantly get worse for your hero. If you come to a 20-page stretch where it's dull, that's probably because your hero isn't in enough emotional or physical jeopardy. And if it gets better for your hero in a particular scene, then the next scene has to make it worse than it's ever been before.

"It also helps to isolate your hero," Holland continues. "One device I use a lot is that nobody believes the hero, who becomes increasingly more isolated from society, friends, family...anyone who can help. It's the isolated hero whom nobody believes is in trouble, and who must finally, reluctantly, rely on his own resources. In THE TEMP, Timothy Hutton thinks his temp secretary (Lara Flynn Boyle) is the one who's doing all the killing, but everyone else thinks she's the best worker they've ever had. So by accusing her, he only invalidates himself further."

Adds writer Joe Eszterhas on the thriller genre, "It's all about suspense levels. There is no greater danger than a lack of suspense when you're doing a thriller. The suspense levels have to be intense enough and deep enough for it to really work. And if your characters have depth, and you drawn them so that you are seeing reflections of their insides, then the suspense will be deeper."

An erotic thriller/murder mystery, BASIC INSTINCT draws its power from the interplay between Nick Curran, a hard-boiled San Francisco detective who used to booze and snort up a storm, and Catherine Tramell, a beautiful, brilliantly manipulative author and bisexual who gets involved with Nick, a prototype for one of her book characters, as a form of research.

Says Eszterhas, "The psychological-psychosexual dynamic is more intriguing to me than the kind of empty picture that dwells on a whole series of physical confrontations. You certainly need physicality, but I am more interested in the psychological games that threaten people at their core. The games are attacks on people's insides, their souls, their psychosexual beings, on their identities in some way. It's far more interesting and subtle than life or death, and I think on a daily basis all of us face those kinds of encroachments...psychologically, and perhaps psychosexually as well."

Of the ambiguous ending to the film, Eszterhas explains, "One of the reasons why Irwin Winkler and I initially pulled out of the picture is that Michael Douglas was very adamant about ending it in a way where he essentially kills her. Michael objected to the fact that Catherine was constantly one-upping him and that there was no redemption. It ended in a very gray sort of way. Paul Verhoeven at that point agreed with Michael, and another writer was brought in. But after four rewrites, they finally realized that the first ending was the only one that works.

"It really startles the audience. What they expect is a blood bath at the end, but what they get instead is a kiss...so it's a mind fuck. The audience laughs and grins as they walk out of the theater because the ending defies everything they've been led to believe by other movies is going to happen. It clearly gives them something that they're taking away from the theater. They're at home mulling it, going over it, going back to see the film. And that means you've given them something that is more than a 2-hour simple diversion. It occupies their thoughts and makes them think."

Moreover, the ending reflects Eszterhas' connection to the character of Catherine. "In some ways I really loved Catherine Tramell. I loved what she pulled off and the way she did it, and I felt that she shouldn't die. I also think that the world is very complex, and people who do this kind of thing and pull it off don't necessarily die. The other reason I didn't want to kill her is because she outwitted everybody, and she did it as a woman with a terrific amount of style and brains. And I didn't want it reduced to a simple morality level where we have yet one more smart, devious woman punished for her sins at the end and killed by a guy."

This brings up an interesting point. In recent years we've seen a spate of thrillers, like BASIC INSTINCT, with female villains: THE HAND THAT ROCKS THE CRADLE, SINGLE WHITE FEMALE, BLACK WIDOW, FATAL ATTRACTION and Paramount's THE TEMP. There's a sense of female empowerment in these films, with metaphorical ties to the feminist movement in society. They strike a public nerve, this new rash of female villains, reversing the stereotype of the classic female victim.

Another feature in psychological thrillers of late is that the protagonist initially trusts and becomes involved with the villain on some level, professionally or personally.

In SINGLE WHITE FEMALE, a young woman takes out an ad and gets just what she wants: a "single white female" who seems like the perfect roommate. In PACIFIC HEIGHTS, a young couple rents the other half of their duplex to a seemingly fine tenant. In FATAL ATTRACTION, a husband is drawn to a strangely alluring woman and asks if she's discreet. Convinced that he can trust her, he embarks on what he thinks will be a one-night stand. In THE HAND THAT ROCKS THE CRADLE, the mother initially trusts the nanny and hires her.

The trick in all of these thrillers is that the protagonists are utterly deceived by the villains at first, as is the audience. The initial setup must therefore be entirely believable, and the villains so convincing, that there would be no reason to suspect that these seemingly nice, normal, intelligent, attractive people are actually psychotic killers.

In creating the villain for THE HAND THAT ROCKS THE CRADLE, writer Amanda Silver explains that she was very interested in the theme of trust, and imbued in Peyton (Rebecca de Mornay) certain character traits found in the villain Iago from

Shakespeare's OTHELLO. "The way that Iago is closest to Peyton," says Silver, "is that she preys on insecurities that already exist in the protagonists. And indeed she has no power at all beyond what the protagonists give her—bringing her into their home and trusting her, believing what she says.

"At one point Peyton instills the fear in Claire (Annabella Sciorra) that her husband Michael (Matt McCoy) is looking at other women. That's an insecurity that already exists with Claire. Peyton also makes Claire believe that her handyman Solomon may be molesting Emma, and Peyton's planting of Emma's underpants in Solomon's tool kit is very much like the handkerchief of Desdemona, the wife of Othello."

It was also important to Silver that Peyton have a very strong motive for her actions: *revenge*. A pregnant Claire is sexually abused by a gynecologist, against whom she brings charges. The doctor, Peyton's husband, commits suicide and Peyton suffers a miscarriage. With her own family destroyed, Peyton then sets out to destroy Claire and assume her position in the family. And the fear for Claire runs deep: not only is Peyton after her husband, but her two children. Says Silver (*Newsweek*, 1/20/92), "It was clear to me the maternal bond is so fiery and so strong that it is one of the hottest buttons you can push."

Silver also imbued the villainous Peyton with certain likeable, sympathetic, empathetic qualities, creating in her a very complex character with moral ambiguities. One minute she's behaving in a sinister fashion and the next we may actually root for her.

Silver was very aware of creating an emotional/psychological bond between Peyton and the audience, which she likens to Hitchcock's PSYCHO. "There's a scene in PSYCHO, right after Bates kills Janet Leigh in the shower, where he wraps her up with the money (he never even sees the money), puts everything in the trunk of her car and pushes the car into a swamp. And the car, which is white, starts to sink and slowly get covered up by the swamp. But just before it gets completely swallowed up, it stops. And what Hitchcock makes you do is say, 'Oh, no. Keep going!' But in saying that, you are colluding with Bates—with the worst villain you could ever imagine.

"I think with thrillers, the audience wants to be taken for a ride," says Silver, "And it's fascinating that you can get an audience to root for the villain, then feel guilty for it a moment later."

Another thriller device is a slow fuse for the villain, which helps build tension and suspense. In CRADLE, Peyton is very calm and controlled for about the first quarter of the movie. It's like the calm before the storm: we know that something bad is about to happen, but don't know when. Suspense builds to such climactic levels that by the time Peyton blows, it's like a volcano erupting.

In FATAL ATTRACTION, little seeds are planted along the way to subtly indicate that Alex may indeed be a bit strange—too strange. We are given several subtle yet telling indications that there is something about her that may warrant suspicion. Her eyes have a mysterious, almost glazed look to them. She lives in a dark, gritty warehouse district. While playing in the park with Dan and his dog, she suddenly turns angry when Dan jokingly feigns a heart attack. Deadly serious, she says her own father died that way, then laughs and says she's joking—when in fact her father is dead. Sexually insatiable and almost violent in her movements, she seems intensely needy and easily hurt, deeply bonding with Dan without really knowing him. All of these things pave the way for the radical change in her character, her suicide attempt the first in a series of shocking turns that serve to peel away the layers of her severely distorted psyche.

As this occurs in thrillers, the villains gradually stripped away of their protective veneer, their vulnerability increases as the levels of suspense and terror are raised. The key is depriving the villains of the very thing they want, thereby heightening their rage, tapping into their fury, and driving them ever closer to the breaking point.

In lesser thrillers, however, the third act is anticlimactic because suspense levels are too low. There is an insufficient build to a lukewarm climax, which absolutely deadens a thriller.

The build is so important, not only structurally but emotionally. A good thriller sweeps us up into the emotional maelstrom of the characters and situation, tying us in knots as it goes.

HORROR: AN INTERVIEW WITH WES CRAVEN

An undisputed master of the horror genre, Wes Craven has written and directed such bone-chilling films as A NIGHTMARE ON ELM STREET, THE HILLS HAVE EYES, THE HILLS HAVE EYES II, SHOCKER, and THE PEOPLE UNDER THE STAIRS. On conceiving the concepts for his screenplays, Craven says:

"I quite often am impelled by something I haven't seen before. I'm really intrigued with the idea of making a movie that breaks new ground. I have found, however, that quite often there is the attitude of what has been successful before, let's do it again. Usually what the studios produce are remakes, sequels, or things that have been done before and just made in a different way. A NIGHTMARE ON ELM STREET took 3 years to find somebody who thought it was interesting enough to finance. Every studio in town passed on it, and New Line Cinema was the only company that really saw some promise in it."

As for the reasons the script was passed on...

"Too weird; something in dreams wouldn't be frightening because the audience would know it was only a dream; too gory; too strange; not interesting enough. It's really...we've not seen this before, therefore it probably won't work and we don't want to risk our money on it.

"On the other hand, I constantly have people sending me scripts or proposing projects that are essentially a little bit of everything that has been done: a little bit of HALLOWEEN, a little bit of A NIGHTMARE ON ELM STREET, a little bit of FRIDAY THE 13TH, a little bit of ALIEN...whatever it might be. I just read them and am instantly bored, and think the audience would be too. So when I set out to make a film, I always ask myself 'Have I seen this before?' And if I have, then I try to avoid it."

I asked Craven about some of the other problems he finds in screenplays sent to him.

"Sometimes there is a deep cynicism in them where women are exploited in a very harsh and ugly way. The central characters aren't sympathetic, ultimately. They're sort of in it for themselves and are unattractive on an ethical and moral level. You don't care what happens to them. You must have characters you really care about, and I find time and time again that that is violated. As a friend of mine said of a particular script: 'Ugly people doing ugly things.' If that's the case, at a certain point the audience will just turn off. They don't care. So I think you must have a central character who has an inner integrity that represents the very best in yourself. And then you must have a very attractive, charismatic, powerful, frightening villain."

Also critical for Craven is a clear, compelling story line that can be verbally summed up in 60 seconds.

"The simplest thing that I've been able to tell writers that I do on any story is that if I cannot tell it in one minute flat as an interesting anecdote, then I think I'm in really deep trouble on the script. I've always been able to do it on my most successful pictures. It should be clear, not overly detailed and caught up in individual story beats. When I was working on A NIGHTMARE ON ELM STREET, I would tell it to friends as: A series of four kids all have the same nightmare on the same night, and realize at school the next day that they've all dreamed about the same man. Within three days, three of them are dead. One is left. She realizes that the man is somebody that their parents had something to do with who's coming back and killing them in their nightmares, and that she can't sleep until she manages to confront him and bring him into her own life where she can do battle with him."

As for the salient ingredients of a horror film, Craven says: "Horror films deal with the forbidden, and you must cross the line of taste, propriety, and what should or shouldn't be spoken in public. You go into those areas where there are deep disturbances in our psyches.

"I have also found that it's very rich material to go into, things having to do with family or family structures. Most of my really strong films, like A NIGHTMARE ON ELM STREET, THE PEOPLE UNDER THE STAIRS, THE HILLS HAVE EYES, are built around dramas that take place within a family.

"When I've thought about it more, and read more about the whole idea of fears and deep-set misgivings, my feeling is that horror films deal a lot with perceptions that were laid down in the first 5 years of our lives, though I wouldn't be surprised if a lot of them come from the first 2 or 3 years of life when we are small, little creatures, very sensitive, very defenseless, dependent on almost monstrously sized human beings: parents, teachers, authority figures who can be very capricious, can be violent, and certainly have our fates in their hands. We must figure out our path through this group of giants. We don't know quite what's out there. We're afraid of the dark.

"There are a lot of fears that exist on a very primal level. Sleep can be terrifying. I remember when I was a child having a nightmare and realizing I had to sleep the next night, and that very primal fear never left my memory. So I go back and explore things that are from the infancy of my own life and the infancy humanity."

On primal fears, Craven says, "In going back to the first five years of life and things that were relevant there, I've found that has a lot of resonance. There are things that take place in bathrooms, which is the first place a child goes where all the mysteries of the body are dealt with. It's the first room where you can lock the door and be separate from your parents. It's where you can submerge yourself in water. There are a lot of very primal things in a bathroom."

As for conceiving and orchestrating his characters...

"I spend a lot time on the characters, and approach any given script as sort of a complex, extensional depiction of the main characters. In other words, besides trying to have a well-rounded central character—for example Nancy in the first A NIGHTMARE ON ELM STREET—I tried to make her very real, give her real friendships and real family issues. Beyond that, I always think of the individual characters who surround the main character as sort of alternative personalities."

In other words, certain parts of the main character's psyche are reflected in the personalities of the other characters.

"So as the stupid person is killed off, the unprepared person, the person who is too prejudiced to seek an ally in a black person...whoever is killed off, those elements of the main character's central personality are stripped away and you end up with sort of a purified character who is prepared to face the worst that life can throw at them.

"In NIGHTMARE, every person that died had certain escape devices that kept them from facing a very painful truth. When Freddy [the villain Freddy Krueger] started making his appearances, the parents who had killed him for molesting children all denied that he ever existed. One parent, Nancy's mother, went into alcoholism. Her father retreated into authority and disbelief. Her boyfriend found solace in food. Her girlfriend resorted to romantic love to deny what was going on.

"All of these people who were killed off were in some form of denial about what was happening. So at the end, Nancy is stripped of all these devices of denial and actually reverses from childhood to parenthood. In the scene right before her final confrontation with Freddy, she actually tucks her mother in bed like a child, becoming a mother to her mother. She essentially arcs through her entire life through the picture.

"I sort of approach it as a single life, and everybody in it will be standing for elements of that life that are there at the beginning and erased at the end by the crucible of events."

As for Freddy Krueger himself...

"One thing I like about Freddy is that he never lies. You always know exactly what he thinks and he does what he says. When I constructed Freddy, basically my intention was to devise the most fearsome adult father , one who hated children and was actually out to exterminate the next generation—which is, I think, a child's worst fear. I set out to make Freddy absolutely frightening and despicable, but also very, very clever. He's adept at moving in the areas of psychology and subconsciousness that most of us are not. That is, dreams and the very well-springs of our consciousness—that are where all the boundaries of civilization and logic are thrown away every night by our minds as we go into something virtually unknown, sort of an oceanic state. So Freddy was devised to be the jaws in the seas of unconsciousness.

"At the same time, there is something very attractive about somebody who is very powerful and is free to express rage and tears away all the phoniness. There's something very attractive about villains in a vicarious sense. Lucifer was depicted as an angel of light, not a slob with long hair and tattoos all over him. The essence of true evil is that it can honestly be attractive and charismatic.

"One of the reasons Freddy was so popular is that he takes away all the parental and authority figures who are full of lies, fatuousness and incompetence by killing them. And to a kid, that's attractive in a symbolic sort of way because they're dealing with a lot of lies and hypocrisy. Parents tell kids to be neat and clean up their rooms, while the kids read in every newspaper that the environment is going to hell and the adult society has been dumping their waste into everything that's pure and turning it into poison. There's a tremendous amount of rage between generations; kids sense a duplicity and a web of lies. So when somebody like Freddy comes along—someone with this absolute cynicism who slashes away at everything, that can be attractive.

"Ultimately the deepest perception I think about when writing a script is that while we do have impulses to be good parents to ourselves and to our children, we're also dealing with our own impulses to be destructive and vindictive. It rolls around in our subconscious...in our dreams and daydreams."

MURDER MYSTERY: AN INTERVIEW WITH WILLIAM LINK

William Link is a prolific, award-winning writer and producer who, with his late partner Richard Levinson, created such classic TV mystery/detective series as COLUMBO, MURDER, SHE WROTE (co-created with Peter S. Fischer), MANNIX, McCLOUD, and ELLERY QUEEN. A supremely accomplished team for many years, Link and Levinson won multiple Emmys,

Golden Globes, five Edgar Allan Poe Awards from the Mystery Writers of America, and the Peabody Award ("the Pulitzer of broadcasting") for their production of the TV film THE EXECUTION OF PRIVATE SLOVIK.

I asked Link: What are the salient ingredients of a murder-mystery?

"In mysteries, you're really not dealing with any kind of heavy-duty character writing. Because mysteries are by their nature manipulative, the characters are like chessboard pieces that the writer skillfully manipulates.

"What people want in mysteries, I have found, is plot. They want to be fooled. In a mystery you've got to unmask a murderer, and you have to be believable in setting up 'whodunit' and why the others didn't. Good mystery writers disguise the murderer very carefully. There was one technique that Agatha Christie used in which she would make one suspect very suspicious, and then the detective would step in and show why that person couldn't have done it. Then the audience dismisses that person from their mind, and at the end that person did commit the murder, but in an entirely different way from what you expect.

"In writing a mystery you're faced with a great deal of logic, whereas you can use the unconscious mind much more in writing a drama. With mysteries you've got to do much harder work consciously because it's all manipulation. You have to use the analytical mind almost all the time in writing a good mystery, unless you want it to be totally implausible and unbelievable."

On what it means to write from the unconscious mind, Link says, "When a writer writes, a lot of it is unconscious. You get it down on paper and get that first draft. Then what comes into play is the analytic mind: this part doesn't work, this is weak structurally, that's got to be fixed up, this must be reinforced, this character is flat and you don't understand his motivation. Here the analytic mind comes into play, and in writing a mystery, it is your companion throughout. In a drama, however, you kick the analytic mind out of the room. You don't need him. He's going to thwart you. Too much analytical thinking in a drama might curtail your freedom to move in certain directions you didn't know about. That's what the unconscious mind allows you to do."

On the subject of detectives, Link says: "I find very few unique detectives now. There's nothing new under the sun, really, but if you can come up with something new, that's all to the good. Columbo was quite unique. He had no family of characters surrounding him, no sidekicks. I think in the entire series you've only seen his office once. You really don't know anything about Columbo. He's a mystery man. He comes out of limbo, solves the case, and goes back into limbo. Dick and I really wanted a character who had no baggage at all, because every other character really did up to a point. They had a backstory.

"You usually don't find much arcing in the detectives. If you take a look at Columbo, he's the same now as he was 20 years ago. It's the same gimmicks, the same shtick, the same pretending to be humble and not that bright when really behind it all this is a brilliant mind at work."

As far as structure, there are two types of mysteries: *open* and *closed*. An open mystery is one in which the audience knows who the murderer is from the beginning but the detective doesn't. So the story becomes a matter of watching the detective crack the case. In a closed mystery, the murderer is unknown to both the audience and detective. For the closed mystery to work, the plotting must be extremely clever and deceptive, never letting the audience in on whodunit until the end.

Says Link, "In a closed mystery, you often have multiple suspects and, what you must strive for is not confusing the audience, which is becoming less and less responsive to complexity of plot. Everything is becoming streamlined now. People don't want to puzzle out clues. It's too complicated for them. The audience has become far less patient of really complex mysteries. There's too much going on in their lives. It's the MTV generation; give it to us quick and we got it, onto the next.

"When we brought COLUMBO back four years ago after it had been on hiatus for ten years, we found through audience research that people really didn't know who the murderer was, and this really confounded us because it's an open mystery. The whole first 20 minutes of every COLUMBO is the murderer committing the murder, but the audience couldn't figure it out. We were thrown for a loop. We realized that all the clues we would set up in the first 20 minutes the audience really didn't pay attention to. They liked the bumbling detective and the humor, and loved Peter Falk as that character. But they didn't really follow the story."

Nonetheless, Link stresses the necessity of telling a good story.

"Many writers do not know how to tell a story. What they do is get a concept and sort of know what the ending is, but they don't have a clue how to get from that first scene to the climax. I think one of the major reasons for this is that most of the young writers don't read. That is a major, major problem. What they do is get all their input from TV or the big screen. I speak at universities all over the United States, and the young writers say to me: How do I learn to write a mystery? And I tell them to read the mysteries of the '30s. Read the Agatha Christies, the John Dickson Carrs, the Ellery Queens. They wrote rather bloodless characters, but their structures were impeccable. Their surprises were wonderful. Their ingenuity was first-rate. You really don't get that anymore.

"Two of our television movies, MURDER BY NATURAL CAUSES and REHEARSAL FOR MURDER were very, very successful and highly rated. They won the Edgar Allan Poe awards as the best of the year. And what these movies had were very interesting concepts and a whole multiple series of surprises with endings that you couldn't see coming. Very clever surprise endings...sometimes multiple, one-two-punch endings in which there are two interlocked surprises. The audience sees one ending, and then suddenly on comes another, which does not invalidate the first ending. These are very hard to structure and few can do it well. In fact, if you asked me to name in this town ten excellent mystery writers, I would be hard-pressed.

"I find a new attitude now of 'who cares?' It's mostly because the writers aren't clever or patient enough to sit down and really work out their clues. On COLUMBO we would sit down and maybe spend a week just on one clue. Now writers don't want to do it. It's too difficult for them. When we brought COLUMBO back, it was so hard to find writers because a good mystery is so difficult to structure. It's much easier to write a car chase show or one that's full of sex, going from bed to bed. That's easier for a writer. You can make the money faster."

Indeed, most of the mysteries I'm asked to evaluate are terribly unsuccessful, failing to keep you guessing throughout. The stories are often so simplistic and transparent that the murderer is easily pinpointed in the first 30-40 pages. There aren't multiple suspects; it's simply a matter of choosing between two possible killers.

Or if you don't know who the killer is, the story isn't compelling enough to make you *want* to guess. Many times the circumstances of the murder are too bland, the writer failing to give us reason enough to care that Frank down at the factory was found in a ditch. Why in the world should we be at all concerned that this character has bitten the dust?

The writer has to draw us into the world of the story and characters, particularly in a mystery. We must have a damn good reason to care that a murder has taken place, and that the story cannot be over until the murder is solved.

As such, prime ingredients include (1) a conceptually striking killing, (2) an intriguing world in which the story takes place, (3) fascinating characters, (4) clever, deceptive, deftly placed clues, (5) an intricate story line which keeps us guessing throughout, (6) a stunner of an ending when the killer is finally revealed, or (7) an ending, like BASIC INSTINCT, which doesn't come right out and tell you exactly who the killer is, but is so thought-provoking in its ambiguity that you can't help but play detective in your own mind to solve the case.

SCIENCE FICTION: RON SHUSETT, DAN O'BANNON

In the sci-fi genre, prominent themes include *space travel* (WHEN WORLDS COLLIDE, FORBIDDEN PLANET, STAR WARS, STAR TREK, THE MARTIAN CHRONICLES), *time travel*

(THE TIME MACHINE, TERROR FROM THE YEAR 5000, THE TIME TRAVELERS, 2001: A SPACE ODYSSEY, TIME AFTER TIME, TIME BANDITS), *depiction of the future* (1984, THE DAY THE WORLD ENDED, THE LAST WOMAN ON EARTH, PLAN-ET OF THE APES, SOYLENT GREEN), and *human vs. alien* (THE WAR OF THE WORLDS, INVASION OF THE BODY SNATCHERS, NOT OF THIS EARTH, THE ANGRY RED PLAN-ET, CLOSE ENCOUNTERS OF THE THIRD KIND, ALIEN, E.T.). (Information from "The Science Fiction and Fantasy Film Handbook" by Alan Frank, Barnes & Noble Books, 1982)

Also prevalent in the genre are space crafts, robots, androids (automatons resembling humans), cyborgs (part man, part machine), lasers, and holographs.

Stories range from the cerebral (THE TWILIGHT ZONE) to the metaphorical (parallels to the Cold War and McCarthyism are often drawn from INVASION OF THE BODY SNATCHERS) to those dependent on action and hardware (TOTAL RECALL).

In the crafting of a sci-fi screenplay, we find that the star element is a highly imaginative *concept*.

Says Ron Shusett, who conceived the story for ALIEN with Dan O'Bannon and executive produced the picture, "Science fiction is driven by high-powered imagination, especially today, since Lucas, Spielberg and Cameron have made such an impact on the public. You damn well better have a high-powered concept to blow the audience's mind or else the MTV generation is going to get bored. What if we had a colony on Mars? What if we could buy an artificial memory? What if an alien life form could grow inside you like an insect? If you're going to label it and advertise it as mind-blowing science fiction, you've got to have the concept. That's inspiration. Then you use not inspiration but craftsmanship to lay in your character—and hopefully soul and humanity, to the degree one has it."

In discussion with writer Dan O'Bannon we delve deeper into the genre, examining the depth of thought and imagination that went into the writing of ALIEN.

In terms of theme, O'Bannon says "The basic notion of astronauts adrift in a remote part of the universe, who touch down on a planet to encounter a threatening foreign life form, is a very classic, archetypal notion in science fiction—even more in literature, I think, than in films, because such films are expensive and difficult to make. The first real science fiction author, H.G. Wells, has a reverse of it in WAR OF THE WORLDS. In that case the dangerous, strange life forms come to earth in their ships. I tapped into all of the related themes of isolation, and the fact that space is eternal night helped quite a bit."

When conceiving the world of the story, O'Bannon "didn't want to randomly create any type of science fiction environment. I wanted to include the elements of remoteness, a great distance from earth—too far away to even consider that you might be able to summon help or escape to earth. The planet they touched down on I wanted to be exceedingly barren and mysterious, so it was perpetually mist-shrouded. You really can't see any distance at all, and anything can hide within the mist. So anything that made it darker, more remote, more isolated, lonely, mysterious and sterile was what I wanted. In terms of the spaceship itself: claustrophobia. The feeling of being trapped in these little corridors, no place to escape. There's an entire universe out there but it's a vacuum. All of that space, rather than being a comforting escape, is an infinity of emptiness all the way down in all directions."

In terms of the story itself, O'Bannon says, "The science fiction movies I enjoyed as a kid had reached a certain point developmentally, and to continue in that vein was no longer novel or interesting. Just to remake THE THING would be a pointless exercise. So I wanted to take it a step or two beyond to really mesmerize the audience.

"But when I first completed the script and began to market it, I wondered whether I created something that was too esoteric for a general audience. Because nobody had ever done anything like that before. They didn't give a damn about the biology of creatures, and I wondered whether this would go over the audience's head. But then Ron Shusett said 'I think the people will go for it because the astronauts are confronted with a basic life or death situation. I think that will grip people and bring the movie into the mainstream.' And that proved to be true."

Indeed, the fact that the astronauts had such a human quality allowed for enormous audience identification with their problem. They weren't just scientific space travelers. They were *real people*. At the same time, however, character depth and complexity are not necessarily a staple of the sci-fi genre.

Says O'Bannon, "In science fiction you're in there for the idea, so it's quite different from a straight character story. And the way that specifically plays out is: In what realistic manner would people respond to an unrealistic situation if it were to occur? You want your characters to be credible to the extent that you can believe them. You want to think about their reactions very carefully and try to guess realistically how people would respond. But generally speaking, the private personality problems the characters have are not relevant because you're not dealing with their inner problems. You're dealing with something external. And too much emphasis on character can undermine the piece. If you go into too much about their inner flaws, you'll simply find yourself writing off the point and the audience will get restive, and rightly so.

"There's a belief in many quarters that all drama must be about human character and its problems, that this is a universal necessity. And it's not true. The notion that every type of drama is or must be about complex, deep, idiosyncratic characters is a dogma, not a fact. Generally in the science fiction genre, deep character is not that important. People need to be credible, and that's about it. In some of my earlier science fiction/horror scripts I wanted to make the characters as deep and interesting as they would be in a straight character piece, but it was just awful. And it took me a long time to slowly figure out that deep character is simply not a universal rule. Some forms of drama are more about ideas than people, and science fiction is a specific illustration of that.

"The creature was the character in ALIEN. It's the alien whose individuality we are interested in, not the people. As conceived, the alien was a hybrid of science fiction and horror. Science fiction is concerned with ideas, the impact of the novel upon humanity. Horror is concerned with frightening the audience. Put them together and you have the impact of the novel to create fear."

O'Bannon says that *fear* is the primary ingredient he tried to inject into ALIEN. He wanted to make the audience scream. He began with the idea that has always appealed to him ("astronauts in deep space encounter a threatening life form"), and then "spent quite a few nights really digging deep down into myself for imagery that I found frightening and repellent to assemble into that creature."

And what really went into the creation of the creature?

"Distorted sexual imagery, body mutilation imagery, some of my phobia of insects, some of my knowledge of the behavior of small biological creatures. Ticks, for example, will wait indefinitely on a leaf, frozen in a sort of suspended animation for years, if necessary, until a potential host animal brushes the leaf. Then they will spring and imbed their proboscis into it. So it was a question of looking closely at my own phobias, trying to render them conscious in my mind, so that I could turn them into a fictional creation that disturbed me. Because one thing I knew is that you really can't frighten an audience if you can't frighten yourself. To try, in cold blood, to intellectually cobble together a frightening story usually doesn't work. I had to have access to my semi-conscious or unconscious feelings. Without them you end up with hack work. Things that are put together strictly from the intellectual surface of your mind have no effectiveness."

In terms of the sexual imagery in ALIEN, it was a key factor in making the creature terrifying.

Says O'Bannon, "Everybody finds sex disturbing to one degree or another, and I have long been fascinated by the notion of alien sexuality. So I thought with a little effort in that direction I could turn it to a very disturbing purpose. I came up with the notion of homosexual rape, and thought I could really get under the audience's skin by having this creature perform oral rape on a male astronaut. I knew darn well how touchy male audiences are on the subject of homosexuality and male rape in general. And I was very surprised in the critical reaction to the film that no one mentioned that. There was plenty of opportunity for critics to notice that the form of attack the alien took was sexual, that it thrusts a phallus down a man's throat. I thought about it and realized that it was a case of cognitive dissonance. It was so bothersome to them [critics] that they couldn't face it. They blocked it out. That didn't cancel out the alien's effectiveness, it just kept it in the realm of feeling. It was too disturbing to acknowledge intellectually, but it was certainly part of what made the alien a disturbing, frightening thing.

"I didn't want to have a female raped by the alien because I thought that was common, obvious and vicious. Filmmakers for a long time have enjoyed brutalizing their female characters, the prettier the better, and to me that was a cheap shot. I didn't want to go that way. Instead I wanted to go after the men in the audience, who are the victimizers."

This also played a part in O'Bannon's choice of a female hero. "I didn't feel any dramatic necessity to put the strength in the men only. I also wrote the script in an era when feminism was beginning to get some recognition at last, and I thought it would be intriguing to show a future in which men and women were genuinely equal in terms of the social tasks given to them. In science fiction films I grew up with, it was standard to have a heroine in danger who's rescued by a man, and it was something I was particularly tired of. So I decided to rattle the audience's expectations by showing the women just as strong and up to the task as the men, and to show the men, if anything, more victimized than the women. I had a desire to unsettle the gender and sexual comfort of the entire film."

In reviewing this chapter, what I want you to come away with is the depth, thoroughness and expertise with which the masters approach their work. Their techniques reflect everything we've learned in this book: the importance of concept, the link between character and plot, the necessity to hook the audience emotionally, the need for credible characters, the importance of keeping the protagonist in jeopardy against a formidable antagonist and sustaining a strong narrative build.

But more than these fundamental strengths in the crafting of a screenplay, we've seen that the genre masters go beyond them into such areas as the reluctant hero, primal fears, creating secondary characters as extensions of the main character, the unconscious mind, tying action into a locale, sexual imagery, and attacks on our psychosexual beings.

The hope is that you will insist upon such depth of thought in your own work, thereby increasing your chances of success.

8

Dialogue

In a standard script submission, it isn't dialogue that will make or break the deal. Dialogue is generally not a primary concern in a screenplay for possible sale. If a project is worth pursuing but the dialogue needs work, another writer can always be brought in. It's not considered an insurmountable problem.

On the other hand, points out writer Leslie Dixon, "All the witty dialogue in the world in a script in which nothing is happening is still going to make them [executives] put it away before they get to the end. All the care you lavish on these witty little exchanges is really the least important thing in a studio's mind."

Where dialogue *is* scrutinized is in a writing sample. Consistently strong dialogue in a script is rare, and writers with that kind of talent definitely stand out. Says Tig Production's Gregory Avellone, "We really respond to great dialogue. If the dialogue is right on—if it's true to character and does more than just advance the plot—we'll tend to be enthusiastic about the writer."

In most of the screenplays I cover, the dialogue is unmistakably average. There may be some bright spots here and there, but nothing is memorable. Sometimes I'll find strong dialogue in a marginal script, but it's rarely the case that a terrific script has substandard dialogue. If a writer can write, the submission usually exhibits strong writing across the board. But if I'm on the fence about a script or a writer, dialogue may ultimately tip me in a positive or negative direction.

PRIMARY FUNCTIONS OF DIALOGUE

The most obvious function of dialogue is communication: an exchange of information between characters.

But because a screenplay is more than just simple communication, dialogue is also used to motivate and justify the actions of a character, create conflict, inject emotion, and reveal exposition (character, plot, backstory, time, place).

—A character learns a piece of information, and is motivated to take action

—A character takes an action that seems out of character, then justifies his behavior by explanation

—A single line of dialogue may ignite a furious argument

—Dialogue can move a character to tears or fits of laughter

—Dialogue regarding a character's past (backstory) can explain or justify his actions today

—Dialogue (speech patterns, word choice) is reflective of and specific to a character

—Dialogue is reflective of certain time periods and locales

DIALOGUE STRENGTHS AND WEAKNESSES

We've touched upon various facets of dialogue in earlier chapters. In Chapter 6 we discussed how a character is best revealed through action instead of blatantly expository dialogue. We learned in Chapter 5 that dull, talky, seemingly directionless dialogue is a structural weaknesses that bogs down the pacing of a screenplay. We delved into subtext in Chapter 4—how the true meaning of a scene is often found in what is not being said rather than the dialogue itself; how the writer can avoid the problem of dimensionless, "on the nose" dialogue, revealing exactly what everyone means, thinks and feels.

But let us refer back to the section in Chapter 2 (WHAT HOLLYWOOD LOOKS FOR IN A SCREENPLAY), which covers some important essentials about dialogue. Major elements include:

BELIEVABILITY: Good dialogue is natural and believable. You don't question the words that come out of the characters' mouths. It doesn't sound forced or mechanical, as if the writer is trying too hard to impress. It's credible and conversational. It doesn't call attention to itself as "movie dialogue."

Says writer Darryl Poinicsan, "A script should be so rooted in reality that you're not conscious that someone has written it. If you come out of a movie saying 'What great dialogue,' the movie didn't work well. The dialogue that actors do best is basically non-dialogue that is believable and rooted solely in behavior. Otherwise, it calls too much attention to the writer."

CONSISTENTLY INDICATIVE OF CHARACTER: Depending on their personality, level of intelligence, ethnicity, age and gender, all the characters in a well-crafted screenplay have their own individual speech patterns. From the words they choose, their level of humor or seriousness, their command of the language and the overall complexity or simplicity with which they express themselves, what your characters say and how they say it is directly tied into who they are.

But, says Universal story analyst Michael Serafin, "A lot of writers will write all their characters exactly the same. Sometimes I can't even tell which character is the male and which is the female by reading the dialogue. Interchangeability in dialogue can do great damage to a script."

Adds executive Cathy Rabin, "Dialogue should be organic to the character. Each character should have a distinctive voice, and while snappy patter and 'bon mots' are fun and appreciated, one has to be careful not to allow glibness to take precedence."

DIALOGUE MUST BE APPROPRIATE TO THE GENRE: When dialogue fits its genre, it adds humor and wit to comedy, emotion to a drama or tension to a thriller. Good writers adhere to certain genre conventions: not relying on dialogue to propel an actioner, or hampering the pace of a sci-fi script with mounds of technical explanation.

Such was the problem with a supernatural thriller I recently passed on, the writer stopping the story cold for lengthy discussions of physics and the cosmos. The plotting became too dependent on dialogue for clarity and explanation, diluting the supernatural angle and working against the grain of the genre.

Says New Regency's Steven Reuther, "If in the middle of a movie the writer has to stop and explain to me where he is, what he's doing and why, something isn't working."

Other major problems include dialogue which is too talky, rambling, nonsensical, hackneyed, stilted, artificial or flat.

Says Gregory Avellone, "In everyday scripts that get submitted, I find that the dialogue is just mundane, not inspired."

Adds story analyst Mark Valenti, "I like invention. I appreciate snappy dialogue." Valenti also advises writers to "thumb through their scripts, and if you see lots of black ink in massive areas, cut it. Learn to kill your babies. Even if you're getting rid of the funniest monologue in the universe, if it's not essential to carry the story forward, cut it."

"Arguably the easiest problem to recognize in dialogue is that it's overwritten," says Universal's Leonard Kornberg. "You rarely hear, 'Oh, it's underwritten,' And make sure that the exposition is dramatized. Don't lay it out in dialogue, which is easy and bad."

As for excessively racist, sexist, vulgar or profane dialogue, nine times out of ten it's speaks negatively of a script. Says story analyst Martha Browning, "I see a lot of that and immediately I'm against the script. The dialogue seems in poor taste. There are ways to be funny without racist jokes and crude sexual references. SISTER ACT never took advantage of Whoopi's color."

On the other hand, a successful use of sexually charged dialogue—and a very good example of good dialogue in general—can be found in the first act of Joe Eszterhas' BASIC INSTINCT. The dialogue is tough, but Eszterhas never reduces it to merely cheap, sexually explicit talk. He relies far more on subtlety, style and humor—as in the initial interrogation of Catherine Tramell...

INT. POLICE INTERROGATION ROOM - DAY

Large, antiseptic. Windows on two walls.

She walks in with Nick and Gus. In the room are Prosecutor John Corelli, Capt. Talcott, and Lt. Walker. A video camera on a tripod records the proceedings.

As soon as she comes in —

> CORELLI
> I'm John Corelli, Ms. Tramell,
> assistant district attorney. I
> have to inform you that this
> session is being taped. —This
> is Captain Talcott...

She offers her hand. They shake.

> CAPT TALCOTT
> My pleasure.

> CORELLI
> And Lt. Walker.

She acknowledges his cool gaze with a nod.

> CAPT. TALCOTT
> Can we get you anything? A cup of
> coffee?

> CATHERINE
> No thank you.

CORELLI
Are your attorneys going to join us —

NICK
(hiding a smile)
Ms. Tramell waived her right to
an attorney.

Corelli and Talcott glance at Nick. She sees the look.

CATHERINE
(smiles)
Did I miss something?

NICK
I told them you wouldn't want an
attorney present.

LT. WALKER
Why have you waived your right
to an attorney, Ms. Tramell?

CATHERINE
(to Nick)
Why did you think I wouldn't want one?

NICK
I told them you wouldn't want to hide.

CATHERINE
I have nothing *to* hide.

The two of them keep their eyes on each other.

She sits down. They sit around her. Nick sits
directly across from her. She lights up a cigarette.

They watch her. She is poised, cool, in complete command of herself.

> CORELLI
> There's no smoking in this
> building, Ms. Tramell.

> CATHERINE
> What are you going to do? Charge
> me with smoking?

Ever so casually, she blows her smoke across at Nick.

INT. INTERROGATION ROOM - LATER

> CORELLI
> Would you tell us the nature of
> your relationship with Mr. Boz?

> CATHERINE
> I had sex with him for about a
> year and a half. I liked having
> sex with him.

She has control of the room: she looks from one man to the other as she speaks.

> CATHERINE
> He wasn't afraid of experi-
> menting. I like men like that.
> Men who give me pleasure. He gave
> me a lot of pleasure.

A beat, as they watch her. She is so matter-of-fact.

                    CORELLI
        Did you ever engage in sado-
        masochistic activity with him?

                    CATHERINE
                    (smiles)
        Exactly what do you have in mind,
        Mr. Corelli.

                    CORELLI
        Did you ever tie him up?

                    CATHERINE
        No.

                    CORELLI
        You never tied him up.

                    CATHERINE
        No. Johnny liked to use his hands
        too much. I like hands — and fingers.

They stare at her.

INT. INTERROGATION ROOM - LATER

Gus closes some blinds to screen out the bright afternoon
light.

                    LT. WALKER
        You describe a white silk scarf
        in your book.

                    CATHERINE
        I've always had a fondness for
        white silk scarves.

(caresses her wrist)
They're good for all occasions.

NICK
But you said you liked men to use
their hands.

CATHERINE
No. I said I liked *Johnny* to use
his hands.
(she smiles)
I don't give any rules, Nick.
I go with the flow.

They have their eyes on each other.

INT. INTERROGATION ROOM -LATER

The sun is low. Harsh light now streaks in through the
other window.

CORELLI
Did you kill Mr. Boz, Ms. Tramell?

CATHERINE
I'd have to be pretty stupid to
write a book about a killing and
then kill him the way I described
in my book. I'd be announcing
myself as the killer. — I'm not stupid.

CAPT. TALCOTT
We know you're not stupid, Ms. Tramell.

LT. WALKER
Maybe that's what you're counting
on to get you off the hook.

NICK
Writing the book *gives* you the alibi.

CATHERINE
Yes it does, doesn't it?

She holds his eyes a second, then —

CATHERINE
The answer is no. I didn't kill him.

INT. INTERROGATION ROOM -SUNSET

GUS
Do you use drugs, Ms. Tramell?

CATHERINE
Sometimes.

She spreads her legs just a bit in Nick's direction.

CORELLI
Did you ever do drugs with Mr. Boz?

CATHERINE
Sure.

GUS
What kind of drugs?

CATHERINE
Cocaine.

She looks directly at Nick.

CATHERINE
Have you ever fucked on cocaine?
(she smiles)
It's nice.

He watches her.

INT. INTERROGATION ROOM - TWILIGHT

NICK
You like playing games, don't you?

CATHERINE
(smiles)
I've got a degree in psychology.
It goes with the turf. Games are fun.

They are holding each other's eyes.

NICK
How about boxing? That's a game.
Was that fun for you?

They don't take their eyes off each other for a second.

CAPT. TALCOTT
I don't think that's relevant to
this inquiry.

CATHERINE
(to Nick)
Boxing was fun. Till Manny died.

NICK
How did you feel when he died?

CATHERINE
I loved him. It hurt.

Their eyes are still on each other. In the distance,
lightning flashes and thunder rumbles.

NICK
How did you feel when I told you
Johnny Boz had died —that day
at the beach?

Lt. Walker switches on some lights.

CATHERINE
I felt somebody had read my book
and was playing a game.

NICK
But it didn't hurt —

CATHERINE
No.

NICK
Because you didn't love him —

CATHERINE
That's right.

Their eyes are digging into each other.

NICK
Even though you were fucking him.

CATHERINE

You still get the pleasure. Didn't
you ever fuck anybody while you
were married, Nick?

A beat; he stares at her, expressionless.

LT. WALKER

How did you know he was married?

CATHERINE

(watching Nick)

Maybe I was guessing. What
difference does it make?

She lights a cigarette. He stares at her.

CATHERINE

Would you like a cigarette, Nick?

He just stares at her, expressionless.

CORELLI

Do you two know each other?

NICK

No.

CATHERINE

(eyes on him)

No.

INT. INTERROGATION ROOM - NIGHT

Outside, it's pouring. Raindrops dribble down the window
panes. Neon signs cast rippling shadows on the walls.

LT. WALKER.
How did you meet Mr. Boz?
CATHERINE
I wanted to write a book about
the murder of a retired rock star.
I went down to his club and picked
him up. Then I had sex with him.

LT. WALKER
You didn't feel anything for him.
You just had sex with him for your book.

She looks at Nick.

CATHERINE
In the beginning. Then I got to
like what he did for me.

GUS
(after a beat)
That's pretty cold, ain't it lady?

CATHERINE
I'm a writer. I use people for
what I write. Let the world beware.

She and Nick have their eyes on each other, then —

CATHERINE
(to Corelli, smiles)
Would you like me to take a lie
detector test?

INT. POLYGRAPH BOOTH - NIGHT

She sits in a bare, windowless cubicle with a polygraph
EXAMINER. The Examiner studies a strip of graph paper

from the polygraph and shuts down the machine. Then he undoes the sensors from her fingertip and arm, and unstraps the belts from above and below her breasts.

> EXAMINER
> Wait here, please.

He rips the graph paper from the polygraph and heads out of the room. She looks straight ahead at the wall.

INT. MONITORING ROOM - NIGHT

On a TV MONITOR, we see Catherine looking directly into the lens. PULL BACK and find Gus, Nick, Lt. Walker, and Talcott watching the monitor in a small office.

The Examiner enters the room.

> EXAMINER
> No blips, no blood pressure
> variations, no pulse variance.
> Either she's telling the truth
> or I've never met anyone like her.

A long beat.

> CAPT. TALCOTT
> (standing, relieved)
> Then I guess that settles it.

Talcott leaves, and the others follow. Nick keeps watching her on the monitor as she lights a cigarette.

> NICK
> She's lying.

Walker stops at the door.

>   EXAMINER
>   Forget it. You can't fool me; you
>   can't fool the machine.

Nick heads out.

>   NICK
>   Trust me — it can be done.

>   EXAMINER
>   And what makes you such an expert?

>   NICK
>   (a beat)
>   I know people who've done it.

Nick and Lt. Walker leave the room.

INT. POLYGRAPH DEPARTMENT - NIGHT

They arrive in the hallway just as Talcott and Catherine
emerge from her booth. She is carrying her things.

>   LT. WALKER
>   Thanks for coming in, Ms. Tramell.
>   I'm sorry to inconvenience you.

She says nothing, has a thin smile.

>   CATHERINE
>   Can I ask one of you for a ride?

They look at her a beat.

NICK

Sure.

CATHERINE
(smiles)
Thanks.

And he and Catherine walk away. Gus and Walker watch them.

A RECAP:
— SHOW DON'T TELL: Avoid long, boring speeches and needlessly wordy exposition
— Each character must have a distinct, idiosyncratic way of speaking
— Good dialogue has subtext
— Good dialogue is crisp, inventive, believable, conversational
— Good dialogue is appropriate to the genre
— Avoid cheap, tastless dialogue.

Afterword

Getting your script through the Hollywood maze doesn't necessitate brilliance. Peruse the movie section of the papers and that fact is more than evident. Still it's damn tough to break into the system. Thousands of hopeful screenwriters bang on that door every year and can't get in. They crank out spec scripts with all the energy they can muster but no one will read them. Or the scripts do enter the system but are stopped at the first rung, never reaching the executives.

But that's the business. And for those who love it enough, you keep on trying because you're driven by passion. You'd take a hundred rejections in the movie business any day over a cushy job with 9 to 5 drones who can't wait 'til Friday. You'd rather make $35 a day in the business than $50,000 out of it. That has always been my philosophy, so bleak is the thought of working in an insurance company or accounting firm just to pay the bills.

In the course of this book you've heard some of the top writers in the industry talk about *passion*. It comes through on the page and people react to it. If you start out from there, you at least have something real going in.

Then you add craft, talent, saleability and drive—and if you've got what it takes, someone is bound to recognize your work. It may happen with your first screenplay; it may take years. But KEEP WRITING. Your next script could be the one that lands you an agent. Your next script could be the one that a story analyst raves about and turns over to an executive. Your next script could be the one that gets bought and made.

Jump into the trenches. Consider yourself a part of the business. Pour everything you've got into the writing of your screenplays, and don't be afraid of failure. Be afraid of abandoning your dreams.

Index

LINDA STUART was on staff at Paramount Pictures for five years, and has read for numerous independent companies such as Sally Fields' Fogwood Films, Meg Ryan's Fandango Films, CAA, American Zoetrope, and Samuel Goldwyn Co. She has recommended such scripts as SNEAKERS, GLENGARRY GLEN ROSS, SECRET OF MY SUCCESS, REVERSAL OF FORTUNE, SCROOGED, and THE WITCHES OF EASTWICK. Ms. Stuart teaches a course in Story Analysis at The American Film Institute. She also works as a private script consultant.